DEVELOP ALONE

12 KEYS TO INNOVATIVE WORK FOR AN AMAZING SOFTWARE RELEASE

ALEX GURKIN

Table of Contents

Preface

Alone or with a team, however you choose to work on a project, one of the main tasks is to get started. I assume that my reader has some competence in programming and is far from deep knowledge in project management. In the book, I will explain the basics of project business models, show how to socialize and delegate some tasks with startup management and use popular success metrics for software.

Key 1. Discover Pros and Cons for Starting a Project Alone

When you're running a software startup on your own, you have to weigh the pros and cons of running the company on your own. While it is possible to work alone, you'll have to be more cautious about growth and the risk of following your own ideologies. Though you can work alone, it is better to have a team. If you're planning to work with other people, you should have a plan that will allow you to share your workload and keep communication open.

Flexibility

Another benefit of starting a software company on your own is the flexibility. A software business is scalable. You can create multiple products with different pricing tiers. You can also work from home and control the workload without the need for expensive office space. A further benefit of a software business is that you can work from home. In addition, you'll be solving real problems for customers, which is what makes it so appealing. You'll also be working on something you're passionate about, which is an added bonus.

Family and friends

You'll spend more time dealing with startup problems than with friends and family. In addition, you'll have to put in more hours to maintain a successful startup. Moreover, you'll have to sacrifice time with your family and friends. Besides, there's the risk that government problems will disrupt your work. If you're an extrovert, you might be lonely working alone with only a houseplant or a book to keep you company.

More time

A software startup is not just a small business. Unlike a traditional business, you'll have to devote significantly more time to the business. And, the rewards of running a software business alone are many. You can work at home, from anywhere in the world, and it's a recession-proof industry. However, if you're not sure whether you want to spend your money on marketing, it might be a good idea to hire someone to do it for you.

Background

While a software startup can be a great opportunity for someone with a technical background, you'll need to be patient and persistent. According to Jeff Lawson, many startups don't make it.[1] However, if you're able to do it, you'll probably have a better career opportunity in the future. And you can always try to hire a team. If you're ambitious, you'll have more options in the future.

Software Development: Working Alone vs. With a Team

When it comes to software development, there are two main ways you can go about it: working alone or with a team. If you're looking to implement your own project and develop the software yourself, then the option of working alone may be suitable in some cases. I have had experience working on software development both as a team and alone, and both of these options have advantages and disadvantages.

10 disadvantages of working alone are:

- ► Loneliness
- ► No one to brainstorm with
- ► No accountability
- ► Can be more difficult to stay motivated
- ► May take longer to complete a project
- ► Can be harder to get feedback and constructive criticism
- ► You may become too attached to your own ideas
- ► It can be easy to get bogged down in the details
- ► There's no one to pick up the slack if you're having a bad day
- ► You may miss out on important skills you can learn from others.

On the other hand, there are also several advantages to working alone such as:

- ► Fewer distractions
- ► More flexible hours
- ► Complete control over the project

- Easier to stay focused
- Can be more enjoyable and satisfying

So, as you can see, there are pros and cons to both working alone and with a team. It really depends on your own preferences and what will work best for your project. When I worked on my first project alone, it was good. When I delegated some tasks it became excellent.

Key 2. Unlock Financial Independence for the Project

If your project now or in the near future is non-commercial, perhaps understanding the future possibilities for monetization will influence the architecture of the software you are currently working on.

I remember a time at the beginning of my favorite project when I was filled with motivation. Back then, turning ideas into a finished product was more important. Back then I put aside business models and sales and just worked. This approach is not loved by startup incubators, but it can be comfortable for some of us. Later, when one of my projects (Friday CRM) came to fruition, I went back and reconsidered what I had written about in this chapter.

How Do You Plan to Charge Your Users?

There are a few different business models and metrics to consider.

1. SaaS
2. Enterprise
3. Usage-Based
4. Subscription
5. Transactional
6. Marketplace
7. E-Commerce
8. Advertising
9. Hardware

Why is SaaS My Favorite Business Model?

SaaS refers to software as a service delivery model. It is software offered by the provider on the web. Customers can access and use the software, typically through a web browser, while the provider manages the infrastructure and security.

The main advantage of the SaaS business model is that it allows for a recurring revenue stream. This means that you can charge your customers on a monthly or yearly basis, which can provide a more stable income for your business.

Another advantage of the SaaS business model is that it is typically very easy to scale. This means that you can add more customers without having to invest in additional infrastructure or resources.

Finally, the SaaS business model can be very profitable. This is because you can typically charge a higher price for your service than if you were offering a traditional software product.

If you're thinking of starting a software business, then the SaaS business model is definitely worth considering.

Why Do Investors Like SaaS Projects?

Even if you, as a startup entrepreneur, are not considering attracting external investment to your project, it's worth noting why investors like to invest in SaaS businesses.

SaaS is a business model in which software is provided on a subscription basis, typically over the internet. SaaS has become a popular choice for investors because it offers a number of advantages.

One reason SaaS is attractive to investors is that it allows for recurring revenue. With SaaS, customers typically pay on a monthly or annual basis, which provides a steadier stream of income than one-time product sales. This predictability can make it easier to forecast cash flow and growth.

Another reason SaaS projects are appealing to investors is that they often have high gross margins. Because there are no physical products to produce and distribute, SaaS companies can keep more of their revenue as profit margin. This can make SaaS businesses more valuable and attractive to investors.

Finally, SaaS businesses often have high customer lifetime values (CLV). Because customers are locked in through recurring payments, SaaS companies can enjoy longer-term relationships with their customers. This can lead to greater customer loyalty and higher profitability over time.

For these reasons, SaaS has become a popular choice for startup founders looking to attract outside investment. If you're considering pursuing a SaaS business model, be sure to keep these factors in mind when pitching to potential investors.

8 Another Business Models and the Metrics Investors Want

This section will cover the key differences between the four most common types of business models and the metrics investors are looking for. Here are the main ones. Listed below are some of the metrics investors will be looking for:

Enterprise

To determine the viability of an enterprise company, you need to know the type of product you're selling and how you measure success. Some of the most popular business models for enterprise companies include subscription-based software, cloud-hosted software, and advertising experiments. The first type of business model requires revenue. For example, a company selling cloud-hosted software will measure revenue by measuring cost paid to acquire customers. The second type of enterprise company requires revenue by measuring gross margin and compounded growth rate.

Another important factor in a successful enterprise business model is the number of paying users. Most investors will want to see metrics that demonstrate growth and retention rates, which indicate profitability. Some businesses have high retention rates, which is one of the most important metrics. Another type of enterprise business model is subscription-based, which enables a company to expand and maintain its customer base over time. A subscription-based business model is an alternative way to grow, while a perpetual model requires ongoing costs.

Usage-Based

Software companies are increasingly turning to Usage-Based pricing as a way to grow their business. This new business model aligns customer spending with their desired outcomes while ensuring that they do not become shelfware. This model is also highly attractive to investors who value committed recurring revenue. Here are some key metrics to watch for in this new type of business model:

Pricing is a key to usage-based pricing. Fixed pricing is easy to recognize for finance departments but can be risky because it can overcharge customers based on usage. Tiered usage-based pricing sets a price at different levels of quantity. Per unit usage-based pricing charges customers for specific quantities of a product, such as the number of active integrations or minutes used on a cellular plan.

Metrics such as customer lifetime value should also be monitored closely. In some instances, customers may stop paying even after using the product. However, this is unlikely to happen if you're using a Usage-Based pricing model. Incentives should focus on ensuring that customers return to your service. But don't forget that your sales force should be compensated based on their commitment.

Subscription

A subscription business model is most valuable when the recurring revenue exceeds the customer acquisition cost. One important metric to measure in subscription businesses is the customer lifetime value, or CLV. This figure shows how much revenue a subscriber generates over a given period of time. The goal is to make that figure larger than the cost to acquire the customer. To calculate CLV, divide the total cost of acquiring a new customer by the total cost of sales and marketing. This ratio will help investors determine whether or not a business is maximizing its revenue potential.

Another metric to measure is the average revenue per user (ARPU). ARPU measures how profitable a product is for subscribers and tells investors about the company's financial health. High ARPU rates suggest a growing market for a product. It can also signal opportunities for cross-selling and upselling. This can also indicate if a company should change its pricing to increase sales. These metrics are critical to the success of a subscription business.

Some of the main advantages are:

- It is a great way to build recurring revenue.
- It helps you to focus on customer retention rather than customer acquisition.
- It encourages customers to use your product or service more frequently.
- You can offer a variety of pricing options to meet different customer needs.

- It helps you to track customer usage and trends over time.
- You can offer additional services or features to subscribers.
- It gives you the ability to upsell or cross-sell other products.
- Subscribers are usually more loyal than one-time customers.
- You can offer a free trial to new subscribers.

Transactional

Among the most sophisticated business models, transactional businesses are a combination of e-commerce and services. The metrics investors want to measure include user growth and lifetime value. This business model is often a good fit for companies that have already proven their ability to attract and retain a large customer base. While there are exceptions, transactional businesses are generally geared toward experienced buyers. To help entrepreneurs choose the right model, here are some tips:

The metrics investors want to know: The first and most basic is lifetime value. This is the best way to measure how much revenue your company has generated since customers will continue to use your services. You can also measure revenue if your company is charging a fee for every single transaction. This can be misleading for startups with spikes in growth, but investors still want to see this number. CMGR is an excellent indicator of overall growth, but you can't base your decision on it alone.

Marketplace

While the number of transactions is important to gauge the health of a marketplace, it can also be a vanity metric. While transactions can be a valuable indicator of the growth potential of a marketplace, they are not actionable. Instead, investors should look at metrics that can prove sustainable growth, such as the ratio of sellers to buyers and the percentage of repeat purchases. In addition, a marketplace's average listing price should provide insight into how much people are willing to pay for its goods and services.

Marketplace founders face challenges while trying to build a scalable and enduring product. One common challenge faced by marketplace founders is the 'chicken and egg' problem, in which the company's customer base doesn't necessarily translate into profitability. To combat this problem, many successful marketplaces have strategically flouted local laws, assuming that their customer base would be large enough to support legal action. As a result, Uber is banned in Bulgaria and Denmark and has been limited in London and NYC. However, this risk-taking stance has been rewarded by the incredible growth of these marketplaces.

E-Commerce

Metrics are essential to any online business, but there are many important differences between SaaS and e-commerce. The most common metrics in e-commerce include sales, cart abandonment rates, customer lifetime value, and churn. In addition, there are a lot more data points to analyze with e-commerce. Nevertheless, these metrics can reveal opportunities and challenges and help you improve your customer experience.

eCommerce businesses are typically considered high-value when they sell products and services that are unique and proprietary. Such businesses generally maintain high-quality marketing through customer reviews, educational content, social media promotion, and paid advertising. However, eCommerce businesses that are dependent on a single source for traffic will generally not command a high valuation. As a result, investors will look for metrics to determine whether your company is a good candidate for growth.

Amazon's success is a prime example of an e-commerce company with a diversified business model. The company has several business units, including an e-commerce platform that sells both its own products and those of third parties. Amazon also offers third-party advertiser services, such as Amazon Prime, which provides faster delivery of goods. The company also provides enterprise cloud services through its AWS platform.

Advertising

As more businesses begin to monetize their content, advertisers want to see the results of their advertising campaigns. One way to measure the effectiveness of advertising campaigns is to look at the paid cost to acquire customers. This is an especially useful metric to monitor when an advertising campaign is unsuccessful. For example, the paid cost to acquire a customer is one of the metrics investors look for when evaluating a company's advertising campaign.

A good example of this revenue stream is the advertising model. Many free websites and apps make money through advertising. For example, Morning Brew, a coffee and lifestyle podcast for business people, sells advertising space to businesses that sell products relevant to the audience. The advertising business model is also very common among media companies like Spotify and Forbes. Many free mobile apps earn money through ads. The key to success in this model is building an audience.

Hardware

The one-and-done business model is simple: create a product, sell it, and move on to the next product. This model is often used in the hardware industry, where new products are constantly being released. The goal is to sell as many units as possible and then move on to the next product.

As a hardware startup founder, you need to understand the fundamentals of building a successful hardware company. Profitability is king, but you also need to understand the metrics investors will look for. For example, a high P/E ratio for a hardware startup will not attract investors, while one with a low P/E will, so you should focus on generating recurring revenue. Growth is also a key metric, but it isn't the only metric.

Most hardware businesses follow the "one and done" model, which means that customers purchase one product and then never buy from the company again. While this approach works fine for many consumer-facing hardware companies, investors often prefer recurring revenue streams and financial viability. This is why LTV is important for hardware companies. You should also consider the recurring cost of retail customer acquisition when calculating LTV. For this reason, recurring revenue is more important for hardware startups than it is for software companies, as also noted by Paul Smyth[2].

Customers' lifetime value is a critical metric for hardware startups. While hardware businesses have a high-margin product, customers tend to feel "technical FOMO" if they cannot upgrade or replace it soon enough. Hardware-as-a-service companies can leverage the lifetime value of each customer by offering software and services. The customer experience must be redesigned around service and data flows. A high-margin company is likely to attract investors, but the metrics investors want should be centered on customer value.

Key 3. Create Business Model Canvas

What is a Business Models Canvas for a Startup? How does it work, what are the benefits and disadvantages of using it, and what are some variations and modifications? Let's start by understanding what the canvas is and why it is valuable to startups. After all, you're in business to build a business, not to copy the model of someone else. So, what can a Business Models Canvas for a Startup do for you?

What BMC Is

Getting a handle on your startup's business model can be an important part of your plan. While you're creating your business model, you need to know your key focal points. These include your products and services, key activities, and key partners. Using a business model canvas is a great way to figure out what matters most to your customers. Once you've got a handle on your focus areas, you can use the canvas to determine the rest of your strategy.

A business model canvas is a tool used by startups to brainstorm and identify potential business models. This tool can be used in conjunction with a traditional business plan to compare various options. Some elements of the canvas can be tested more easily than others. Some, such as customer segments, are more easily testable than others. If you want to test different scenarios, you can use A/B testing. To test your assumptions, you can use a free web tool called Canvanizer.

PAIN ↓	SOLUTION ↓	VALUE PROPOSITION ↓	RELATIONSHIPS ↓	CUSTOMER SEGMENT ↓	CHANNELS ↓
		KEY METRICS ↓	RESOURCES ↓	KEY PARTNERS ↓	
	COST STRUCTURE ↓			REVENUE STREAMS ↓	

Table A. My version of the modification of the BMC

Every business faces unknown risks. By utilizing a business model canvas, you can identify those gaps and create a nuanced strategy. As your business grows, the canvas becomes a scorecard for you and your team. You may want to adjust your business model as customers make feedback. By creating a business model canvas, you'll have a better idea of what customers want and how you can best deliver that.

Advantages of Using BMC

When starting a startup, the importance of developing a strong business model cannot be overemphasized. A well-designed business model can give you a better understanding of your competitors' business models and give you a clearer insight into the operations of your startup. As you develop your business model, you'll be better prepared to generate cash and expand your business to new markets. The advantages of using a business model canvas for a startup are numerous. By connecting value propositions, revenue stream, and customer segmentation, you can create a business model that is both scalable and sustainable.

One of the major benefits of using a business model canvas is that it breaks down your business model into logical segments. For example, the Value Proposition focuses on the product or service you're offering. By separating the product or service into logical segments, you'll be able to create a more accurate picture of your customer base. This way, everyone involved in the business can understand the direction of the startup.

Another advantage of using a business model canvas is that it can help you identify key partners to provide value to your customers. These key partners will help you develop relationships with and ensure consistency for your customers. Lastly, the Business Model Canvas helps you test the impact of your revenue stream on the bottom line. While Lean Canvas focuses on the what, the business model canvas dives deeper into the how. By using both types of canvas, you can quickly see how each piece fits together.

Disadvantages and Criticisms

While conventional wisdom says that the Internet is a fertile ground for disruptive business models, the traditional business model remains an unproven option for startups. While Google Inc. and Daimler AG have been criticized for their failures, the former has built a promising new venture in car2go, one of the most successful car-sharing companies in the world. Disadvantages and criticisms of business models for startups vary, but there are some key characteristics that most successful startup businesses share.

Variants and Modifications

There are various forms of the Business Model Canvas. It is a concept that allows a high degree of complexity in describing the functions of a company. Generally, the Business Model Canvas has nine basic building blocks. These elements cover four of the most crucial areas of a company. The HOW section of the business model canvas illustrates the company's revenue model and cost structure. It also provides a clear idea of the company's stakeholders and key resources.

Some aspects of the Business Model Canvas are easier to test than others. The key activity is to determine the value proposition for the customer. This activity should be differentiated from competitors and provide value to customers. This value can be achieved by the various elements of the Value Proposition. These elements may include risk, convenience, usability, and accessibility. The value proposition is then achieved through key activities.

Key Blocks and Their Descriptions

Here is a list of the key blocks for a business model's canvas.

- ▸ Customer Segments: who are your customers?
- ▸ Value Propositions: what do you offer to your customers?
- ▸ Channels: how do you reach your customers?
- ▸ Customer Relationships: what kind of relationship do you have with your customers?
- ▸ Revenue Streams: how do you generate revenue from your customers?

A Business Model Canvas is an outline for a startup's strategy. It can help you determine the focus areas of your business, such as what your customers really want. You can break your business model into different categories such as customers, resources, activities, and key partners. The key activity should be directly related to your value proposition.

If you're not sure how to go about building this structure, here are a few tips.

First, break the business model canvas into its component parts. Once you've done that, you'll be ready to map out new ideas. To do that, you'll need to break the canvas into key blocks and analyze each one. Gather the stakeholders that are most important to your company and discuss the key blocks of the model canvas. You may want to use sticky notes to organize your ideas around the canvas.

Once you've determined the key blocks of the model, you'll need to consider costs. These costs come in many different forms, but you must focus on cost-efficiency as a top priority for any business. By doing so, you'll be able to clearly articulate what makes your business model so important. You should also consider what customers value most. You should be able to offer them something different than their competitors.

Frequent Questions and Answers

The business model canvas is a tool that helps

entrepreneurs and startups develop a comprehensive model for their business. Ash Maurya developed this method, which is a problem-focused approach based on one-page models. It consists of nine components, including revenue streams, customer segments, value propositions, cost structures, and key activities, resources, and relationships. It is also available as a free downloadable template.

The idea of a Business Model Canvas is to make sure the underlying assumptions are sound and that revenue is greater than cost. The Canvas tool helps entrepreneurs spot holes in their thinking and clarify why something won't work. However, Blank suggests that there are several levels of the Canvas, and that there is no single level that is the same for every business. Here are the frequently asked questions and answers to the tool.

It helps entrepreneurs generate innovative ideas and map potential changes, and it also helps to align team members' goals with actions. By using the BMC, founders can also determine how to attract funding. It also helps entrepreneurs to identify the resources they need to grow and create a sustainable business.

Key 4. Avoid the 5 Biggest Challenges When Growing a SaaS Business

Developing a new SaaS business model is no small challenge. Not only must you find new ways to promote your product or service, but you must also be aware of the growing competition in the market. This means that you must be careful about using old strategies that worked in the past. Since many SaaS businesses are trying new tactics and strategies, you may have to learn a few new ones as well.

Marketing

Unlike tangible products, software services cannot be

held, felt, or smelled. Marketing them is a challenge that requires creativity, particularly since there are no tangible products to be marketed. The SaaS industry is filled with fierce competition, so finding new ways to showcase their value is imperative. Here are five ways to market your SaaS business successfully:

Finding your target audience and targeting them. While data is useful for creating an ideal customer profile, it is not enough to reach consumers. Marketing your SaaS offering to a niche market is more likely to yield leads that fit your model and convert them into paying customers. Marketing your product to your target audience is as difficult as figuring out how to reach them. For instance, Michal Sadowski's company aimed to reach Polish-based business professionals and then sent 2,000–3,000 ultra-personalized messages to them.

Sales

When you're building a SaaS company, sales is one of the biggest challenges. Sales leads are generated by marketing, but closing those deals requires a strong sales team. Sales and marketing teams need to work together to achieve the same goals. Here are five of the most common challenges in SaaS sales. Using sales metrics to guide your marketing strategy and improve your closing rate will ensure you are maximizing your sales.

My book is not about sales, although you will find the first steps on how to bring a product to fruition here. I discovered new things about software sales by studying the books of Jean Rosato[3] and Paul Goodwin[4], which may be useful to you after a successful release.

Internationalization

Although SaaS companies are a complex breed, the internationalization process can be easier than you might think. The very nature of a SaaS business means that it has a global culture ingrained in its DNA, making it easier to scale internationally than other types of businesses. But there are some challenges to consider before extending your SaaS offering internationally. Here are four to avoid.

One of the biggest challenges when expanding a SaaS business is getting customers in other countries. Many companies make the mistake of ignoring the need to expand internationally. This is a common mistake in

European tech companies, which had more venture capital and ambitious founders. While international expansion is great for growth, it requires the translation of content and product to reach new markets. Nonetheless, it's well worth the investment.

Costs

When you are in the early stages of building a SaaS business, one of the most important metrics to consider is your cost of customer acquisition. Although this type of business does not require much reproduction, you should still invest in marketing and lead generation campaigns to compete with existing businesses. As a result, the cost to acquire a single customer will often be much higher than the average for a startup. Read on for some tips to reduce these costs.

COGS is the cost of sales, which includes the costs associated with manufacturing, sourcing, and delivering your product to your customers. This cost is also known as the cost of revenue because it is part of the total cost of goods sold. Some SaaS companies record costs as payroll and hosting fees, which are also included in COGS. These costs contribute to the creation and delivery of your product and include direct labor, raw materials, overhead, and inventory storage.

Lead generation

One of the most important components of your marketing strategy is lead generation. Since your SaaS business is subscription-based, your lead generation efforts will go to waste if you don't nurture them. Your ROI will be very small because your lead will likely churn after a month. Hence, it is crucial to understand your customer journey and develop marketing strategies to appeal to them.

When generating leads for your SaaS business, you can use comparison pages. Buyers will compare different SaaS solutions to find out what suits them best. By creating comparison pages, you can showcase your unique selling points and generate ready-to-close leads. The comparison page should highlight the most significant differences between your products and competitors. In addition, your landing pages must include pricing information and a signup page that prompts a meaningful action.

Key 5. Explore Teambuilding Opportunities

Single founders have certain advantages. They enjoy increased flexibility and are accountable for all decisions. However, they can make strategic mistakes. They can also have difficulty outsourcing product development. As a result, single founders can experience poor decision-making. Here are some advantages and disadvantages of starting a software startup alone. Read on to discover whether being an entrepreneur is right for you. Also, keep in mind that working for yourself is not for everyone.

Single Founders Enjoy Flexibility in Decision-making

A recent study conducted by McKinsey & Company reveals that single founders are more likely to make good decisions than co-founders do. The problem arose from the need for consensus among founding teams. Common knowledge bias, polarization, and conformity pressures all contributed to poor team decisions. According to the study, over 500,000 hours are wasted by managers in Fortune 500 companies on ineffective decision-making. While co-founders are valuable to a software startup, they can make better decisions as a solo.

Single founders often benefit from flexibility in decision-making because they don't have to share equity with other members of the company. They are also more likely to take on more risk than their co-founders. This increased risk-taking can create opportunities and a better company, but it can also lead to problems, especially in the early stages. Having less accountability can also make single founders less likely to have a "single" mindset.

Founders Can Outsource Product Development

Startup founders often face the same roadblocks when it comes to product development. Outsourcing partners have the experience to guide a software startup through the process. Startup outsourcing companies have the experience to translate business models and product ideas into technical requirements. These professionals can also help startups decide which features, technologies, and product development plans will be most effective. By outsourcing their product development needs, a software startup can save time and energy while achieving a robust product.

Before hiring an agency, a software start-up should carefully consider its outsourcing needs. One of the most significant challenges is in the beginning of the project. Clients must clearly outline their expectations, including the context of the market, target users, and the value they are looking to provide. Clear communication between client and outsourcing partner helps avoid potential development potholes. Outsourcing partners should also have a thorough knowledge of the final output.

When outsourcing product development, startups can

focus on other aspects of their startup. The remote team can focus on product development, including evaluating the market, conducting a SWOT analysis, and making recommendations. They can even develop a roadmap to show how the product will progress. After all, product development is a complex process and requires many different skills. However, startups can outsource this task to a development company specializing in the industry.

While hiring in-house employees may be an option, outsourcing can also reduce the startup's expenses. Hiring in-house developers can be expensive, and outsourcing vendors offer ready-made resources. Outsourcing vendors can reduce hiring time by months or even weeks. A startup can also outsource software development to a company that specializes in the specific skill they need. This is an effective solution for software startup founders with limited resources.

The biggest disadvantage of outsourcing product development is giving up control. Outsourced teams may work for other companies or projects while you are working on your project. Outsourced teams are often working for many clients. In-house teams are dedicated to one startup and work together within the same physical space. Because of this, they have full control over product development. The development team can choose which resources to hire and can also hire part-time resources if needed.

How to Build a Team for Software Startup From Scratch

You have a vision for your software startup. Your team must share that vision. You should hire passionate, cross-functional team members who are genuinely interested in your product and the company. Then you can hire in-house developers, specialized engineers, and passionate cross-functional team members. This section explains the process of hiring the right people for your startup. It's not an easy task, but it's not impossible.

Step 1. Hiring In-house Developers

While outsourcing offers a lower price-quality ratio and fewer hiring headaches, hiring in-house developers for a software startup has its advantages. In-house teams are typically located in the company's office or a hybrid work-from-home environment and use company resources. In-house employees are easy to communicate with and respond to questions quickly. In-house developers are also more familiar with the company's culture, so they are likely to be a better fit for the company's mission.

In-house development may be the better option for a startup. The time and money spent on recruitment and onboarding new employees are significant, especially for startups. However, it takes less time to find the perfect partner. If you're still unclear about your product's mission, hiring in-house developers may be the best way to go. Hiring an in-house developer also saves time and effort on other aspects of product development.

As with any project, hiring developers with the right skills and experience can result in a high-quality, unique product. It's important to choose programmers who are willing to work in a team environment and share your vision. To find the right developer, you'll need to screen applications, conduct interviews, and conduct pre-employment tests. This will help you determine which developers are the most compatible with your business's culture.

If you're looking for in-house developers for your startup, it's vital to have a solid funding foundation for your project. Solid funding will allow you to pay your developers well, keep turnover to a minimum, and ensure productivity is high. The key is to find app developers who share the startup's culture and work style. Otherwise, hiring in-house developers can quickly turn into a huge drain on your resources.

Investing in hiring in-house developers has many advantages, but can also be expensive. Hiring in-house developers requires long-term employment, onboarding, and training, as well as managing the employees and paying them based on hourly rates. Not only will it cost you a lot of money, it will also delay the time to market of your project. The downside to hiring in-house developers for your startup is that you need to hire the right team members and keep them on the team.

Step 2. Hiring Specialized Engineers

When hiring for a software startup, cultural fit is often the deciding factor. You want to hire someone who can mesh well with your team and believe in your product. If an engineer believes in your mission, he or she is more likely to thrive in the role and stay with the startup. The following are some considerations to make when hiring for a software startup. Make sure you have a stellar pitch ready to win over the best candidates.

The best candidates are fresh out of college and may not have a lot of experience. This makes it easier for them to make a sacrifice on stellar pay in exchange for a chance to build something unique and important. In addition, millennials often value purpose over dollars, so you should try to recruit from a pool of young graduates. While the pay may not be top-notch, they are eager to make a difference in your company.

One of the most important factors in hiring a software engineer for a software startup is his or her skill set. Software developers with specific domain expertise and different qualifications will ensure that your team has the best possible chances of succeeding. They will be more likely to work together to deliver a high-quality product and minimize the risk of setbacks. If you aren't able to hire a full-time engineer, you can always use freelance engineers who can help you with the project.

If you aren't sure about whether or not an applicant is a good fit for the position, it helps to ask non-technical questions about their interests and hobbies. This way, you can gauge whether the developer will fit with your culture and values. In any case, it is better to hire someone than to risk your project by hiring the wrong person. While hiring specialized engineers for your software startup is a critical part of the success of your business, it doesn't have to be difficult.

Step 3. Hiring Cross-Functional Team Members

Hiring cross-functional team members is an excellent way to maximize the potential of your software startup. Not only will they bring fresh perspectives to your project, they can help you identify strengths and weaknesses that would otherwise be hidden. They can also strengthen your camaraderie with your team members and build relationships with vendors and customers. Here are some tips for hiring cross-functional team members. Let's get started. We'll discuss the key considerations for hiring cross-functional team members.

A lack of communication within the team can lead to inefficiency and poor performance. When cross-functional teams lack communication, they tend to prioritize their own departments over the overall project. In addition, they may not have the same standards for performance and will pass blame off to others. In addition, members may not feel ownership toward the project, resulting in ambiguity and subpar performance. A lack of communication can create a culture of low standards, ineffective collaboration, and low employee engagement.

Having multiple roles allows you to leverage your employees' strengths to complete more tasks. If you're hiring for a specific position, consider asking someone who excels at it. This way, they will feel like they belong and will fit in. You may even hire several people in one department who are great at different tasks. That way, you can use the skills of one team member for another. This way, you can maximize your startup's potential and boost your revenue.

A cross-functional team can help your company fight groupthink. When people within the same department work on the same project, they tend to overlook problems that need to be addressed or old assumptions that need to be challenged. Hiring cross-functional team members can keep everyone in the loop and make critical decisions faster. They can also improve your customer experience by bringing in different perspectives from different departments. The result? A better product.

If you're looking for a cross-functional team, consider using an online collaboration tool like Pingboard. This tool makes it easy to search for specific team members and add custom fields where you can enter their contact information. The org chart can be referred to throughout a project. You can also give peer recognition to specific team members. With Pingboard, you can also easily see when team members are out of the office.

Step 4. Hiring Passionate Team Members

Hiring passionate team members for your startup is an important part of the process. The right people can make or break your business. A company's success depends on the people it employs, and you cannot train people to have the right attitude. If you are a software startup founder, the right people can make your startup run smoothly. Here are some tips for hiring passionate team members:

First, look for a team with diverse backgrounds. The best candidates will often look for their next opportunity through their network. You can use the recommendations of current team members as a gold mine. A happy employee will tell their friends and family about their experience with your company. So, start looking for these candidates as early as possible. You can also create a shortlist of regular co-workers. If your company offers flexible working hours, your team will grow rapidly.

Second, look for founders who have experience in the technology space. Make sure you find people with ten years of experience or more. They should have been involved in software development, managed teams, and created innovative products. As the startup founder, you should act as a technology decision maker, deciding on technologies, front-end development frameworks, programming languages, and more. Founders should also be flexible and strategic.

The best way to motivate your team is to let them know that their work is important and that it contributes to the success of the company. Make sure that everyone understands the company's vision and what their role is in achieving it. Celebrate successes together and reward employees for a job well done. Lastly, keep communication open and let your team know that their input is valued.

Key 6. Get More with a New Co-founder

While it may seem easier to work on your startup alone, it is important to have someone with an additional set of skills. A cofounder can help you make difficult business decisions and provide you with an additional perspective.

A co-founder will also expand your network and help you build a more robust business. It is very important to have the right mindset when looking for a co-founder. It will make the process of building a business much easier and stress-free.

Having a co-founder can help you validate your startup idea, get feedback, and hold you accountable.

A Co-founder Can:

- ▸ be someone to bounce ideas off of, and can help you when you're feeling stuck
- ▸ help with the financial burden of starting a business
- ▸ help with the day-to-day tasks of running a business
- ▸ be a sounding board for your business decisions
- ▸ provide emotional support during the ups and downs of entrepreneurship
- ▸ be a source of motivation and inspiration
- ▸ help you expand your network
- ▸ bring complementary skills and knowledge to the table.

When choosing a co-founder, make sure they have similar skills and temperament. It is very important that they share the same vision and mission. If you are incompatible, you are bound to have problems, especially if the cofounder does not share the same values. A self-sufficient co-founder will reduce the risk of power struggles. In addition to compatibility, having similar work styles is important.

While finding a co-founder for your startup may seem like a daunting task, there are many ways to make the process easier.

Before you begin your search for a co-founder, think about your strengths and weaknesses. Think about your network and industry events. Find people who share your vision and thoroughly vet their credentials. Some people find co-founders naturally. Others may purposefully search for a co-founder. Whatever the reason, it's important to find the right person for the job.

Where to Find a Co-founder for Your Project?

StartHawk is a popular networking platform where you can meet co-founders who share your skills and experience. It matches you with other users with additional knowledge and skills and helps you find investors, mentors, consultants, and partners. The site also has a directory of entrepreneurs, and you can post information about your startup and find other potential co-founders. If you're looking for someone with a technical background, Indie Hackers is a great place to look.

You can also attend startup events around the country, such as BarCamps, where you can meet other like-minded people.

Finding a co-founder for your business is easier than you may believe, as there are so many entrepreneurs using Facebook and LinkedIn to promote their companies.

- LinkedIn
- Facebook Groups
- Slack Communities
- Startup Events
- Accelerators and incubators
- Meetups
- Online forums
- Co-working spaces
- Friends and family

The search for a co-founder is not an easy task, but if you can continue working without one it's best to conduct your own parallel process of finding partners. This could be very unpredictable like all human interactions and processes involving people in general.

Before Hiring a Co-founder

You've finally decided to start a business, but are you unsure about who to hire as a co-founder? Then you need to know whether or not you can work together well. This section will cover some questions to ask a potential co-founder to determine whether their values align with yours. If their values don't match yours, you may want to consider hiring another co-founder.

Tip 1. Find a co-founder whose values align with yours

You can use networking to find a co-founder who shares your vision and shares your values. Join groups on LinkedIn that focus on startup and entrepreneurship, and use their job board to find potential co-founders. Joining a premium community will help you find people with specific skill sets and backgrounds that match yours. The best way to find people to co-found your company is to be transparent about your values and vision.

A co-founder with complementary skills and temperament is a great addition to any team. If you are an engineer or consumer product designer, you need to find a co-founder with a strong business and design background and a non-designer with technical skills. A co-founder who is detail-oriented and organized will complement your creative style. You should also be comfortable discussing ideas and concerns.

When choosing a co-founder, consider whether your values will mesh. Founders typically possess audacity, optimism, and a healthy ego. While co-founders may clash on some aspects of the company, having the same values will make you more likely to work well together. However, if you and your co-founder's visions do not line up, you will be continually butting heads over the direction of the company.

When you're looking for a co-founder, make sure that the two of you have a good rapport. Unlike a partner or best friend, you'll be spending more time together than with any other person. Ensure that you can communicate openly, enjoy conversations, and trust each other to make the best decisions for the company. Your co-founder should be a good person with a solid character.

Before selecting a co-founder, you should identify your superpowers. Be brutally honest with yourself about your weaknesses. Once you've determined your strengths, identify your weaknesses and seek out the one who shares them. If your co-founder has these skills, he or she is the perfect co-founder for you. If they don't, they might not be right for your startup.

Tip 2. Test your relationship with a potential co-founder

When hiring a co-founder, you must make sure that you have a good working relationship with them. You need to feel comfortable talking to them and discussing ideas with them. You also need to know their financial status and personal details. You should be comfortable discussing sensitive topics. However, don't forget that a co-founder can be the most valuable asset of your company, so you must make sure you like them.

The type of relationship you establish with your co-founder is critical to the success of your business. In addition to the skills and knowledge that you bring to the table, you need to feel comfortable communicating with each other. Having a good relationship is essential for a successful partnership, but co-founders can also affect your work environment and personality. If you don't like your co-founder, you should find someone else.

It is important to find a co-founder with whom you share core values. Shared core values are important for your business because they drive how you conduct your business. You should make sure that the two of you are in sync when it comes to managing your team and brand. This is more important than sharing common interests. Though you may share similar interests, you should look for co-founders who have complementary skills and a similar network.

A potential co-founder should have similar work styles and communication styles. Make sure you understand each other's schedules and communication styles before hiring one. If one co-founder works traditional hours, you may have a difficult time getting along. Likewise, if your co-founder has irregular hours, it may be difficult to work together. Be sure to discuss potential conflicts with your prospective co-founder, and come to an agreement on how to solve them.

Before hiring a co-founder, try to have a couple of intense bonding experiences. Working on a high-pressure collaborative project together is more effective than a coffee date. Consider living together for a while or shipping a small product with your new co-founder. In the end, write down your peak productivity as a duo. You'll soon realize if it's a good fit for your company.

Tip 3. Test your commitment to your company

Before deciding to hire a co-founder, it's essential that

you know how well you work together. While chemistry is important, you also want to make sure that you and your co-founder have the same work ethic and values. You can test this by working with each other for a provisional period. After all, if your co-founder doesn't want to be part of your company, you may have to rescind the offer.

If your co-founder is your friend, look for a teammate who has similar commitment levels to yours. If you have families, discuss when the two of you will have time to spend with them. Discuss how you will handle adverse circumstances, as this will strain your partnership. When in doubt, have a backup plan in place to prevent problems from arising. In some cases, it may be a good idea to take a break for a while before hiring a co-founder.

If you are not certain that your co-founder has the same commitment level as you do, write down the specific qualities that you want in a co-founder. For instance, if you are looking for someone who will take charge of the company's marketing, then you can ask them if they have any special talents or abilities. If they don't, seek advice from trusted friends and ask them what their ideal co-founder would be. Use the job description as a metric.

Tip 4. Avoid hiring a co-founder whose values don't match yours

When choosing a co-founder for your startup, you should consider his or her commitment level. You should never hire a co-founder who doesn't share your values. A co-founder will be one of the first employees of your business, and as such, their commitment to your business will be essential. However, every circumstance is different. In order to avoid hiring a co-founder whose values don't align with yours, you should ask each potential co-founder for a personal Capbase account.

When hiring a co-founder, be sure to define the role each will play in your business. This includes defining time commitments, salaries, and voting rights. It is also important to document these agreements early in the company's life cycle. For example, Dorr recommends using OKRs and KPIs to determine responsibilities. This way, there will be no misunderstandings later on.

If the founders have different backgrounds and expertise, it's important to choose someone who knows their industry. A fintech SaaS startup may have a co-founder with experience in platform integration, while an online bank might specialize in blockchain tech or automated payroll. If they don't share the same values as you, it could spell disaster for your business. The co-founder's personal and professional values should be in sync.

Finding a cofounder is not an easy task. It's better to conduct this process in parallel with development because it can be unpredictable like all human endeavors involving people- which means you'll need some luck on your side.

As I mentioned earlier, it is not necessary to build a team, distribute roles and manage the project. However, one person acting as a mini-corporation with an understanding of your own areas of competence and tasks will make it easier to delegate anything when you're ready for it.

Key 7. Stay on Top of Project Management

When starting a software development project, the first step is always to define the project. This may seem like a simple task, but it's actually one of the most important steps in the entire process. Why? Because if you don't know what you're trying to achieve, it's impossible to create a successful outcome.

Define the Project

There are a few key elements that should be included in every project definition:

1. The problem that the project is trying to solve. This is the most important part of the definition, as it will guide all subsequent decision-making.

2. The goal of the project. What do you want to achieve? This should be specific and measurable.

3. The scope of the project. What will be included, and what will be excluded? This is important to define upfront so that there are no surprises later on.

4. The timeline for the project. When do you need to have it completed? This is critical for planning purposes.

5. The budget for the project. How much money do you have to spend? This will dictate what is possible and what is not.

6. The risks associated with the project. What could go wrong, and what are the consequences? This is important to consider so that you can plan for contingencies.

By taking the time to properly define the project before beginning any work, you will set yourself up for success. Without a clear understanding of what you're trying to achieve, it's all too easy to get sidetracked and end up with a result that doesn't meet your needs. So take the time to do it right from the start, and you'll be glad you did.

Why Do Projects Fail?

There are many reasons why projects fail, but some of the most common include:

1. Lack of clear objectives. If you don't know what you're trying to achieve, it's impossible to succeed.
2. Lack of planning. Failing to plan is planning to fail. Without a detailed plan, it's very difficult to stay on track and achieve your objectives.
3. Lack of resources. If you don't have the right people or enough money, your project is doomed from the start.
4. Scope creep. This is when the scope of the project starts to expand beyond what was originally agreed upon. It's important to keep a tight grip on scope creep, as it can quickly spiral out of control and lead to total failure.
5. Poor communication. If people are not on the same page, it's very difficult to make progress. Make sure everyone involved in the project knows what is

expected of them and that they understand the overall plan.

6. Changes in leadership. If there is turnover in the leadership of the project, it can be very disruptive and lead to a loss of direction.

These are just some of the most common reasons why projects fail. By being aware of these risks, you can put yourself in a much better position to succeed.

In reality, projects often fail because of a combination of factors. It is rare for a project to fail due to just one cause. More often, it is a combination of several different factors that leads to a project's downfall.

By being aware of the most common causes of project failure, you can put yourself in a better position to avoid them. By taking the time to properly plan and communicate, you can increase your chances of success. And by being prepared for the worst, you can be sure that you're ready for anything.

Project Constraints

All projects are constrained by time, budget, and scope. These are the three most important factors to consider when planning a project, as they will have a direct impact on what is possible and what is not.

- ► Time: How much time do you have to complete the project? This will dictate the pace at which you work and how much can be accomplished.
- ► Budget: How much money do you have to spend? This will impact the scope of the project and the resources that are available.
- ► Scope: What is included in the project, and what is not? This will define the boundaries of the work and help to prevent scope creep.

Two Types of Projects and Life Cycles

As you learned in the previous step, software development is the process of creating a piece of software that meets the requirements of a customer or client. In order to do this, developers must first understand the needs of the customer or client. Once these needs are understood, developers can begin to create a plan for how the software will be developed.

There are two main types of software development

projects: greenfield projects and brownfield projects. Greenfield projects are brand new applications that have never been developed before. Brownfield projects are existing applications that are being modified or extended.

Each type of project has its own unique challenges and risks. Greenfield projects may be more complex, as they require the development of an entirely new application. Brownfield projects may be less complex, but they come with the risk of introducing errors into an existing application.

Both types of projects also have different life cycles. Greenfield projects typically follow a linear-waterfall life cycle, while brownfield projects usually follow an iterative-agile life cycle.

The linear-waterfall life cycle is a straightforward approach to software development. It begins with the gathering of requirements, followed by the design phase, implementation, testing, and finally deployment. This life cycle is typically used for large projects that are not expected to change much over time.

The iterative-agile life cycle is a more flexible approach that allows for changes and modifications throughout the development process. It begins with the gathering of requirements, followed by a series of iterations in which the software is developed and tested. This life cycle is typically used for smaller projects that are expected to change over time.

The choice of life cycle will depend on the type of project being developed. Greenfield projects are usually best suited to the linear-waterfall life cycle, while brownfield projects are usually best suited to the iterative-agile life cycle.

No matter which life cycle is used, there are four main steps that must be completed in order to successfully develop software: requirements gathering, design, implementation, and testing. These steps will be discussed in more detail in the following sections.

Linear-Waterfall Life Cycle

The linear-waterfall life cycle has the advantage of being simple and easy to understand. It is also well suited to large projects that do not require frequent changes. However, the linear-waterfall life cycle has the disadvantage of being inflexible. Once the software moves from one phase to the next, it is very difficult to make changes. This can lead to problems if the requirements change during the development process.

The linear-waterfall life cycle is best suited to projects that have well-defined requirements and are not expected to change over time.

Iterative & Agile Life Cycles

The iterative-agile life cycle is typically used for smaller projects that are expected to change over time.

The iterative-agile life cycle has the advantage of being more flexible than the linear-waterfall life cycle. It is also well suited to projects that are expected to change during the development process. However, the iterative-agile life cycle has the disadvantage of being more complex and difficult to understand.

The iterative-agile life cycle is best suited to projects that are expected to change during the development process.

Linear & Iterative as Coupled Cycles

The linear-waterfall life cycle and the iterative-agile life cycle can be used together to develop software. These life cycles are typically used for large projects that are not expected to change much over time.

The hybrid life cycle has the advantage of being more flexible than the linear-waterfall life cycle. It is also well suited to projects that are not expected to change during the development process. However, the hybrid life cycle has the disadvantage of being more complex and difficult to understand.

The hybrid life cycle is best suited to projects that are not expected to change during the development process.

System Development Life Cycle (SDLC)

The system development life cycle (SDLC) is a framework that describes the steps that are taken in order to develop a software system. The SDLC includes the following phases: requirements gathering, design, implementation, testing, and deployment.

The SDLC has the advantage of being well-defined and easy to understand. It also provides a clear roadmap for the development process. However, the SDLC has the disadvantage of being inflexible. Once the software moves from one phase to the next, it is very difficult to make changes. This can lead to problems if the requirements change during the development process.

The SDLC is best suited to projects that have well-defined requirements and are not expected to change during the development process.

Vertical AND Horizontal Slices in Agile Software Development

In order to successfully develop software, it is important to understand the difference between vertical and horizontal slices in agile software development.

Vertical slicing is a technique that is used to break down a project into smaller, more manageable pieces. This can be done by breaking the project down into tasks, features, or user stories. Vertical slicing is often used in agile software development.

Horizontal slicing is a technique that is used to break down a project into smaller, more manageable pieces. This can be done by breaking the project down into tasks, features, or user stories. Horizontal slicing is often used in waterfall software development.

The advantage of vertical slicing is that it allows for a more iterative and agile development process. The disadvantage of vertical slicing is that it can lead to a lot of wasted time if the requirements change during the development process.

The advantage of horizontal slicing is that it allows for a more structured and waterfall development process. The disadvantage of horizontal slicing is that it can lead to scope creep and can be very inflexible if the requirements change during the development process.

Both vertical and horizontal slicing have their advantages and disadvantages. It is important to choose the right technique for the project at hand. If the requirements are well-defined and are not expected to change, then horizontal slicing may be the better option. If the requirements are likely to change during the development process, then vertical slicing may be the better option.

What Is Scrum?

If you still choose the path of teamwork, then Scrum comes in handy. It is a framework that emphasizes a structured approach to teamwork, coupled with the principles of transparency, continuous improvement, and clear communication. The basic elements of scrum are roles, artifacts, and activities.

- ▶ Chris Sims and Hillary Johnson recommend that teams work in one-week sprints, devoting one to two hours to sprint planning, no more than 15 minutes to daily standups, one hour to story time, 30 to 60 minutes to sprint review, and one to two hours to retrospective.
- ▶ Understanding Scrum and using its tools effectively is facilitated by Agile values: people and interaction, a working product, collaboration with the customer, and a willingness to change are important.
- ▶ Scrum is all about continuous product and process improvement.

- Scrum provides many opportunities to get feedback from the business customer, the team, and the market and use it to improve. Experience is the best teacher: Doing the work in one sprint, you learn something that helps you plan the next one.

- The roles in a scrum team are divided as follows: product owner, scrum master, and team member. No fourth role is given, nor is it reduced to two.

- Scrum artifacts make the team's efforts transparent. Experts refer to product backlog, sprint backlog, task burn chart, task board, and readiness criteria as artifacts.

- The basic rhythm of a scrum is the sprint period, lasting from one week to one month. The shorter the sprint, the more often the team provides potential product growth and the customer has more choices about when and what to deliver to users or customers.

- Sprint activities include sprint planning, daily scrum, story time, sprint review, and retrospectives.

- The purpose of the retrospective is to identify one or two strategic changes that need to be made in the next sprint to improve the process. In the case of a sprint crash, this is especially important.

What Is a Stakeholder?

A stakeholder is a person, group, or organization that has an interest in the success or failure of a project. The stakeholder can be either internal or external to the organization.

Internal stakeholders are those who are directly involved in the project, such as the project manager, team members, and sponsors. External stakeholders are those who are not directly involved in the project, but who nonetheless have an interest in its outcome.

The stakeholder can be either positive or negative. A positive stakeholder is one who wants the project to succeed. A negative stakeholder is one who wants the project to fail.

Identifying stakeholders early on in the project is important. It allows the project manager to develop a good working relationship with the stakeholders and manage their expectations.

Stakeholders can have a significant impact on the success or failure of a project. It is important to identify them early on and to manage their expectations throughout the project.

How to Create the Perfect Stakeholder Management Plan?

There is no one-size-fits-all answer to this question. Every project is different and will require a unique stakeholder management plan. However, there are some general tips from experts[26],[27] that can be followed to create a successful stakeholder management plan:

1. Define the roles and responsibilities of each stakeholder.

2. Identify the goals and objectives of each stakeholder.

3. Develop a communication plan to keep all stakeholders informed of the project's progress.

4. Manage expectations by setting realistic goals and timelines.

5. Be prepared to deal with conflict should it arise.

6. Regularly review the stakeholder management plan to ensure it is still relevant and effective.

The stakeholder management plan is a crucial part of any project. By following these tips, you can create a successful plan that will help ensure the success of your project.

Change Management Plan

Change management is the process of planning, executing, and monitoring changes to a project. It helps to ensure that changes are made safely and effectively, without jeopardizing the success of the project.

A change management plan is a document that outlines how changes will be implemented and monitored. It should include a description of the change management process, as well as roles and responsibilities for all stakeholders.

The change management plan should be created early on in the project before any changes are made. It should be reviewed regularly and updated as needed.

By following these tips, you can create a successful change management plan that will help ensure the success of your project.

5 Critical Steps in the Change Management Process.

1. Create an Environment for Change

2. Develop a Vision and Plan for Change

3. Make the Changes

4. Incorporate the Changes into Company Culture and Practices

5. Examine Results and Analyze Them

The change management process is a critical part of any project. By following these five steps, you can ensure that changes are made safely and effectively, without jeopardizing the success of the project.

Project Monitoring and Control

Project monitoring and control is the process of tracking, regulating, and managing a project to ensure that it is completed on time, within budget, and to the required standards.

There are several best practices for project monitoring

and control:

1. Use the right tools: There are a variety of different tools available to help with project monitoring and control. Choose the right tool for your needs.

2. Meetings with stakeholders: Hold regular meetings with stakeholders to keep them updated on the project's progress and to get their feedback.

3. Set up project parameters: Define what success looks like for the project and create measurable goals and objectives.

4. Manage scope creep: Make sure that scope creep does not occur by tightly controlling the project's scope.

5. Make forecasts and budgets: Create realistic forecasts and budgets to ensure that the project stays on track.

6. Be flexible: Be prepared to adapt the plan as the project progresses.

7. Find exceptions: Look for deviations from the plan and take corrective action as needed.

8. Make the project engaging: Keep stakeholders engaged in the project by making it interesting and relevant

to them.

By following these best practices, you can ensure that your project is completed on time, within budget, and to the required standards.

It is important to monitor and control projects because doing so can help to ensure that the project is completed on time, within budget, and to the required standards. Additionally, monitoring and controlling the project can help to identify any risks or issues that may arise and take corrective action to prevent them from jeopardizing the success of the project.

Key 8. Take Advantage of Proper Documentation

Documentation is a crucial part of any software development project. By following these tips, you can create effective documentation that will help ensure the success of your project.

1. Make an inventory of what documents you will need.

2. Determine crucial information for each document.

3. Write effective technical documents.

4. Organize your thoughts.

5. Time to test.

Make an Inventory of What Documents You Will Need

In software development, effective technical documentation is essential for two primary reasons: first, it can help developers quickly understand the code they are working on; second, it can act as a reference for future changes or updates to the code. Good technical documentation can make the difference between a well-functioning piece of software and one that is plagued with errors and incompatibilities.

Before you start writing documentation, it is important to make an inventory of what documents you will need. This will vary depending on the project, but some common types of documentation include:

- Product documentation: Describes the features and functionality of the product.
- Process documentation: Describes the process that will be used to develop and deliver the product.
- Data and privacy compliance documentation: Describes the data and privacy compliance requirements for the project.

- ▸ Emergency plans: Describes the plans for dealing with emergencies that may arise during the project.
- ▸ Visual documentation: Creates a visual representation of the project, which can be helpful for understanding complex concepts.

Once you have a list of the documents you will need, you can start to determine the crucial information for each one.

Product Documentation

Product documentation is a type of documentation that describes the features and functionality of a product. It is important to create clear and concise product documentation so that users can understand how to use the product. Additionally, product documentation can help to ensure that the product is used correctly and consistently.

It should be clear, concise, and easy to understand. It should also be well-organized and structured in a way that makes information easy to find. In addition, product documentation should be kept up-to-date as the product evolves.

There are two main types of product documentation:

1. System documentation should provide an overview of the system, its components, and how they work together. It should also include detailed information on the system's architecture, design decisions, and source code. In addition, system documentation should be updated regularly as the system changes.

2. Document kinds such as PRD, Source code document, User Experience Design documentation, Software architecture design document, Maintenance and help guide, and API are examples of these.

User documentation should be written in a clear and concise manner. It should also be easy to navigate and include step-by-step instructions for using the product. User documentation should be updated as new features are added to the product.

User documentation consists of user guides, troubleshooting manuals, installation instructions, and reference tutorials.

PRD — Product requirement document — a type of system documentation

A product requirement document, or PRD for short can be seen as an overview of the system's features. They are used by companies to communicate their vision and functionality clearly with stakeholders so that everyone is on board before starting any work in earnest - this way there won't come confusion later down the road when deadlines approach. A good rule thumb would have you update your documents every time something major changes about either one (a feature). It may seem like common sense, but make sure this gets implemented early enough because, otherwise, things might get out of control halfway through the project[5].

PRDs consist of three main sections:

1. The product overview provides an overview of the product's features and functionality.
2. The project objectives section defines the project's goals and objectives.
3. The project scope section outlines the project's deliverables and milestones.

PRDs are living documents that should be updated as

the product evolves. It can take on different formats such as user stories, functional specifications, or even just rough exploration documents to inform those creating them of what needs added/ changed in future revisions - this will help keep everyone involved up-to-date with progress.

A good understanding is needed before starting off so ensure you have a clear vision for your project.

Here are the most important items you should include in your requirement for the product document:

1. Roles and responsibilities. Begin your document by introducing the details about the project's participants, including the product's owner as well as team members and other stakeholders. These details will define the roles and also communicate the release objectives for each of the team members.

2. Business goals and team goals and objectives. The most important goals should be defined in a succinct form.

3. Background and strategic alignment. Briefly explain the purpose of your action. What are the reasons you are creating the product? What are the implications of your actions on the product's

development and are they in line with the business's objectives?

4. Hypotheses. Create a list of assumptions, either business or technical, that your team could have.

5. User stories. List or link the user stories you need to complete the project. The user's story can be described as a piece of writing that is written from the point of an individual using your software. The user story is a brief outline of the customer's actions and the results they wish to attain.

6. Acceptance requirements. These are the criteria that indicate that a story of a user has been completed. The reason for acceptance criteria is to establish an acceptable outcome for an application scenario from the viewpoint of the user.

7. Design and user interaction. Link the design explorations as well as wireframes to the webpage.

8. Answers. As the team resolves issues along the course of work there will be a lot of questions that arise. The best practice is to keep a record of all the questions and keep track of the answers.

9. Don't do it. List the things that you're not doing right now but plan to complete in the near future. A

list like this will assist you in organizing your team's work and help you prioritize aspects.

The best way to go about it is to draft a requirements document that follows an identical template that the entire team follows. One web-based form can make sure that the document is short and reduce the time required to find the data.

Visual documentation — type of system documentation

User Experience Design documentation is a type of documentation that creates a visual representation of the project. This can be helpful for understanding complex concepts. This will help to ensure that users can understand the project more easily.

UX design starts in the stage of requirements and continues through all stages of development, which includes the post-release and testing stages. This process of UX design involves research prototyping, usability testing as well as the actual designing phase, where a lot of documents and deliverables are developed.

The UX documentation can be broken down into stages. The research stage comprises:

User Personas are developed and documented at the time of the research phase. The data collected during interviews with users and surveys are then compiled into user personas that can be used. Personas for users are the primary features of real-world users, with a focus on their behavior as well as thought patterns and motivation.

User scenarios are documents that describe the steps a user will take to accomplish a task. users' situation is a piece of paper that outlines the steps that a persona will follow to complete an objective. User scenarios concentrate on the actions a user is expected to perform, not outlining the process of thinking. The scenarios could be narrative or visual and can describe existing scenarios or future capabilities.

Scenario maps are used to consolidate the various user scenarios available into one document. Scenario maps show all possible scenarios available at a given moment. The primary reason for the scenario map is that it will present the various scenarios that could be possible for every function, and also intersecting step-by-step scenarios.

A User Story Map is constructed out of backlogs for the application. This kind of document is used to arrange the user's stories into the future functions or sections that comprise the app. The user story map may be a plan or list of stories organized in a specific arrangement to identify the essential features for a particular period of time.

The UX style guide — type of system documentation

The UX style guide is a document that outlines the design guidelines for the upcoming product. It also lists all the possibilities for UI elements and types of content employed and outlines the rules for how they'll be laid out and interact with one another. However, unlike the UI Style guide, UX developers don't provide a description of the design and feel of the user interface.

At the point of prototyping and designing the prototype, the UX designer typically works with documents that are delivered and updated at the same time as the other team members like the product manager, UI designers, and the development team. Dominic Myers points out in his book[6] that documents that are most commonly produced in six stages:

► Site maps
► Wireframes
► Mock-ups

- Prototypes
- User flow schemes or user journey
- Usability testing reports

Quality assurance documentation

Agile user acceptance testing is a process whereby software is tested in short, regular cycles to ensure that it meets user requirements. This type of testing is typically done by the development team, with input from stakeholders and users.

The aim of agile user acceptance testing is to identify any issues with the software as early as possible so that they can be fixed before the software is released to users.

There are different types of user acceptance testing in agile that are distinguished by experts[7]. The most common are:

- Quality management plan: A quality management plan outlines how the project will ensure that the software meets all relevant quality standards.
- Test strategy: A test strategy outlines the approach that will be taken to testing the software.

- Test plan: A test plan outlines what tests will be carried out, and when they will be carried out.
- Test case specifications: Test case specifications detail the individual tests that will be carried out, and what input data is required for each test.
- Test checklists: Test checklists are used to ensure that all tests are carried out and that they are carried out correctly.

User acceptance testing is an important part of the software development process, and it is essential that all stakeholders are involved in the testing process. By involving stakeholders early on in the testing process, any issues with the software can be identified and rectified before the software is released to users.

Process Documentation

Process documentation is a type of documentation that describes the process that will be used to develop and deliver a product. Additionally, process documentation can help to ensure that the project is completed on time and within budget.

The most common examples of process documentation

include project plans, project reports, meeting minutes, and correspondence.

Process documentation should be clear, concise, and easy to understand. It should also be well-organized and structured in a way that makes information easy to find. In addition, process documentation should be kept up-to-date as the process evolves.

There are two main types of process documentation:

- ▶ Operational documentation should provide an overview of the process, its components, and how they work together. It should also include detailed information on the process's inputs, outputs, and risks. In addition, operational documentation should be updated regularly as the process changes.
- ▶ Technical documentation should provide an overview of the technical aspects of the process, including detailed information on the process's hardware and software requirements. Technical documentation should also be kept up-to-date as the process evolves.

Both operational and technical documentation are important for understanding and managing a process.

Process documentation should be created and maintained by the process owner.

The primary distinction between process and product documentation is that the former documents the development process, while the latter depicts the finished product.

Project plans, estimates, and schedules are important tools for managing a software development project. They help to ensure that the project is completed on time and within budget. Additionally, these documents can help to identify and resolve potential problems before they occur.

Project reports provide a high-level overview of the project's progress and performance. They can be used to identify trends and issues, and to make decisions about the project's direction.

Metrics are a type of data that can be used to measure the performance of a process or system. They can be used to track progress, identify issues, and make decisions about the project.

Working papers are documents that provide detailed

information about the project's progress. They can be used to communicate information to project team members and to provide a record of the project's progress.

Agile product roadmaps

A strategic roadmap is a document that outlines the high-level goals of a project, and the steps that need to be taken to achieve those goals, the experts note[8]. It can be used to communicate the project's direction to stakeholders and to ensure that everyone is working towards the same objectives.

A technology roadmap is a document that outlines the technology requirements of a project, and the steps that need to be taken to achieve those requirements. It can be used to communicate the project's direction to stakeholders and to ensure that everyone is working towards the same objectives.

A release plan is a document that outlines the schedule for a project, and the steps that need to be taken to release the project on time. It can be used to communicate the project's direction to stakeholders and to ensure that everyone is working towards the same objectives.

How to Write Good Documentation?

There is no one-size-fits-all answer to this question, as the best way to write documentation will vary depending on the project and the audience. However, there are some general tips from me and contemporary developers[9],[10] that can help to make your documentation more effective:

1. Use simple language

When writing documentation, it is important to use clear and concise language. Additionally, it is important to use language that is appropriate for the audience. For example, if you are writing documentation for a technical audience, it is important to use technical language. However, if you are writing documentation for a non-technical audience, it is important to use simpler language.

2. Be clear and concise

When creating documentation, it is important to organize your thoughts. This will help to ensure that the documentation is clear and concise. Additionally, organizing your thoughts will help to ensure that you include all of the important information in the documentation.

3. Use diagrams and illustrations

When writing documentation, it is often helpful to use diagrams and illustrations. This is because they can help to make complex concepts easier to understand. Additionally, they can help to make the documentation more visually appealing.

4. Use lists and tables

When creating documentation, it is often helpful to use lists and tables. This is because they can help to organize information and make it easier to understand. Additionally, they can help to make the documentation more visually appealing.

5. Be consistent

This means using the same format and layout throughout the document. Additionally, it means using the same terminology and abbreviations throughout the document. Consistency will help to make the documentation more understandable and easier to use.

6. Use templates

This is because they can help to ensure that the document is well organized and consistent. Additionally, templates can help to save time when creating documentation.

7. Test your documentation

Once you have created the documentation for a project, it is important to test the documentation. This will help to ensure that the documentation is accurate and that users can understand it. Additionally, testing the documentation will help to identify any errors or inaccuracies in the documentation.

Creating documentation for a software development project is a lot of work. However, it is worth the effort. Documentation can help to ensure that the project is successful and that users can understand the product. Additionally, documentation can help to ensure that the project is compliant with all relevant laws and regulations. So, do yourself a favor and create clear and concise documentation for your next software development project.

8. Use cross-links

To give your users the right understanding of a subject, use cross-links between documents. For example, if you are documenting product pages or user guides, proper navigation is important to help people follow along without getting lost.

9. Write just enough documentation

It is important to provide the reader with enough information so that they can understand what the software does and how to use it, but you don't want to overwhelm them with details.

10. Consider your audience

When writing documentation, it is important to keep your audience in mind. Ask yourself who will be reading the documentation and what their level of expertise is.

11. Don't ignore glossaries

A Glossary is a list of terms and their definitions. Including a glossary in your documentation can be helpful for readers who are not familiar with all the technical jargon.

12. Keep your software documentation up to date

As your software evolves, so should your documentation. Regularly update your docs to ensure that they are accurate and reflect the latest changes.

13. Involve all members of the team

The success of your documentation depends on the involvement of everyone on the team. Make sure to solicit feedback from all team members and welcome input from everyone.

14. Hire a tech writer

If you don't have the time or resources to write documentation yourself, consider hiring a professional tech writer. They will have the skills and experience needed to produce high-quality documentation.

TOP 10 Tools for Software Documentation and Tracking

The following is a list of the top 10 tools for software documentation for software development projects:

1. Confluence – this software will enable your team to create, collaborate, and organize all of your project's documentation in one place.

2. Jira – project management software will assist your staff in planning, tracking, and releasing your project's source code.

3. Bitbucket – this tool lets your team code, collaborate, and create applications together.

4. GitHub – the version control tool you choose should be able to keep track of changes to your code.

5. GitLab – this program will help your staff manage, plan, and track the development of your project's software process.

6. Redmine – to help your staff manage, track, and plan their software development project, they'll use this

program.

7. Trac – will help your team track the progress of their project and handle its issues.

8. Phabricator – this tool will enable your staff to track, collaborate, and release their software project.

9. Trello – with this program, your team will be able to manage and track their project's activities.

10. Asana – will assist your staff in planning, tracking, and managing their efforts.

This fundamental principle of an agile approach should also be taken into consideration when it comes to the process of creating software documentation. The best software documentation should be made available, whether it's an official document on specifications for software testers and programmers or manuals for the end-users.

It isn't required to create the complete list of documents mentioned within this section. Instead, you should concentrate on the documents that directly aid in achieving the project's goals.

Key 9. Act Quickly from Idea to Growth

The development of your startup, from idea to growth, can be divided into six key phases. A successful startup must go through all of these stages in order to achieve long-term success.

1. Idea phase is the first phase. This is when you have a great idea for a new business and you start to develop it. You need to validate your idea and make sure it is something that people want or need. This is also the phase where you start to put together a team to help you with your new business.

2. Development phase. This is when you start to build your business. You will create a product or service and start to market it. This is the phase where you

need to generate revenue and start to grow your business.

3. Expansion phase. This is when you start to scale your business. You will expand into new markets and continue to grow your customer base. This is the phase where you need to invest in growth so that you can continue to scale your business.

4. Maturity phase. This is when your business has reached a stable point and is no longer growing at the same rate as it was in the previous phases. You will still need to invest in your business, but at this stage, you will focus on maintaining your current customer base and ensuring that your business is profitable.

5. Decline phase. This is when your business starts to decline. This can be due to changes in the market, competition, or other factors. At this stage, you need to focus on turnaround strategies so that you can revive your business.

6. Exit phase, the sixth and final phase. This is when you sell your business or close it down. This is the end of the journey for your startup, but it doesn't have to be the end of your entrepreneurial career. You can use what you've learned from your startup

to create a new one or invest in someone else's business.

If you want your startup to be successful, it's important that you go through all six of these phases. Development is a key in each stage, so don't neglect any stage in the development process.

Product Market Fit

As the product development leader, it's your job to find product market fit. This means creating a product that people want and are willing to pay for. And while market research can help you understand your target market, it's not going to help you find product market fit.

The best companies create their own markets. They don't try to fit into an existing market; they create a new one. And to do this, you need to find a hidden need. Something that people don't even know they want or need.

If the solution is obvious, then lots of people will be doing it. So you need to look for something that's not obvious. In the book by Tim Leung[11], an author I respect, there is a good question to ask yourself on this subject— What jobs are people using your product to do?

And finally, you need to look at where your customers are pulling you. You shouldn't be pushing your customers; they should be pulling you. Look for how users are hacking your solution to do something you haven't thought of. That's where you'll find your product market fit.

Finding product market fit is one of the biggest challenges you'll face as a product development leader. But it's also one of the most rewarding. So don't give up; keep looking for that hidden need.

What Problem Should Your Project Solve?

The development of your project should focus on solving a problem. By identifying and targeting a specific problem, you can create a product or service that meets the needs of your target market. This focused approach will help you to better understand your customers and their needs, which in turn will result in increased sales and profitability.

In order to determine what problem your project should solve, you can use market research and customer feedback to identify potential areas of opportunity. Once you have identified a problem that your project can solve, you can begin developing a solution. This process will require research, development, and testing in order to create a product or service that meets the needs of your target market. By following these steps, you can build your own project that solves a real problem for your customers.

Who is Your Customer?

One of the most important things to think about when starting a business is who your target customer is. Without a clear understanding of who you're trying to reach, it will be difficult to create a successful marketing strategy. There are a few different ways to go about finding your target market.

First, consider what problem your product or service is solving. Who is most likely to need a solution to this problem? Once you've identified your target market, you can begin developing marketing strategies specifically for them.

Another way to find your target customer is to think about who your competition is targeting. If you can identify their target market, you can position yourself in a way that makes you appealing to those same customers.

Finally, consider your own personal development journey. What were some of the biggest challenges you faced when starting out? Who do you wish had been there to help you through those challenges? This can give you some insight into who your target market should be.

Once you've identified your target market, you can begin developing marketing strategies specifically for them. This might include creating targeted content, running ads on specific channels, or partnering with other businesses that serve similar audiences. DBy taking the time to identify your target customer, you'll be one step closer to building a successful business.

For some types of audiences for my client projects I had to apply special strategies. For example, I have been using advice from Adam Duvander's book[12] to attract developers as users.

If you're not sure where to start when it comes to identifying your target market, consider working with a marketing consultant or development coach. They can help you create a plan specifically tailored to your business. And if you need help with the execution of your marketing strategy, they can also connect you with the right resources.

Building a successful business starts with understanding who your target market is. By taking the time to identify them, you'll be one step closer to achieving your goals.

Why is Too Wide an Audience Bad for a Project?

Project development is a process of trial and error. The more people that are involved in this process, the greater the chance that something will go wrong. Too wide an audience can be bad for a project because it increases the chances that someone will not like what the project is doing and will give up on it.

A project should focus on a small group of people at first and then gradually expand its audience. This way, the project can get feedback from a smaller group of people and make sure that it is doing what they want.

Are Potential Consumers Willing to Pay?

As a development team, it's important that you think about how your target market perceives the value of your product or service. You need to consider whether potential consumers are willing to pay for what you're offering. If they're not, then you need to find a way to adjust your business model so that they are.

There are a few ways to go about this. First, you can try to increase the perceived value of your product or service. This can be done by improving the quality of what you're offering, or by adding new features that consumers will find valuable. You can also try to reduce the price of your product or service so that it's more affordable for potential consumers.

Finally, you can try to find a niche market that's willing to pay for what you're offering. This can be done by targeting a specific group of people with your marketing, or by tailoring your product or service to their needs.

If you can't seem to make any headway with potential consumers, it might be time to rethink your business model. Sometimes, the only way to find success is to try something new. So, don't be afraid to experiment until you find a model that works for you and your target market.

Making the Project Visible

The development of your project is important, but if potential consumers cannot find you, it does not matter how great your product or service is. You need to make sure that your project is visible and easy to find online. There are a few ways to do this:

- Make sure your website is optimized for search engines. This means using the right keywords and phrases and having quality content.
- Use social media to your advantage. Create accounts on popular platforms like Twitter, Facebook, and Instagram, and post regularly.
- Advertise. Invest in some online advertising to make sure potential consumers are seeing your project.
- Use the sites as Betalist, Appsumo, and Product Hunt

Which Customers Should You Go After First and Second?

The development of your business will be greatly accelerated if you focus on acquiring the right type of customer from the start. When it comes to choosing which customers to go after first, there are a few things you should take into account. First and foremost, you should identify your target market and who your ideal customer is. Once you know this, you can start to look for customers who fit this profile and who are likely to be interested in your product or service.

There are a few other factors to consider when choosing which customers to go after first. For example, you should think about which customers are most likely to use your product or service on a regular basis and who are most likely to recommend it to others. You should also consider which customers are most likely to be profitable for your business in the long run.

Once you have a good understanding of who your ideal customer is, you can start to focus on acquiring them. There are a number of different ways to do this, but one of the best methods is to create content that is targeted at your ideal customer. This could be in the form of blog posts, eBooks, white papers, or even just helpful articles on your website. By creating content that is relevant to your target market, you can attract them to your business and build a relationship with them.

Once you have acquired some initial customers, you can start to focus on acquiring more customers in a similar way. However, you should also start to think about ways to retain the customers you already have. This can be done by providing excellent customer service, offering loyalty programs, and making it easy for customers to recommend your business to others.

Does Your MVP Actually Solve the Problem?

The development of your MVP is crucial to the success of your project. It is important to ensure that your MVP actually solves the problem that you are trying to solve. Otherwise, it will be difficult to gain traction with customers and investors.

There are a few things that you can do to ensure that

your MVP actually solves the problem:

- ▸ Define the problem that you are trying to solve as clearly as possible.
- ▸ Research your target market and understand their needs.
- ▸ Create a prototype of your MVP and test it with potential customers.

If you take the time to develop a well-thought-out MVP, you will be in a much better position to succeed with your project. Don't rush the development process and make sure that your MVP actually solves the problem that you are trying to solve. Otherwise, you will likely find yourself struggling to gain traction down the road.

Is It a Good Idea to Start with a Low Price?

If you are starting a business, development or otherwise, do not automatically discount or start with a super low price. You may think that this is a good way to attract customers and get business, but in the long run it will hurt your bottom line.

Discounting devalues your product or service in the eyes of the customer. If you are constantly discounting, customers will begin to think that your product or service is not worth full price. This can lead to a decline in sales and revenue.

Super low prices can also be a sign of poor quality. If your product or service is priced too low, customers may think it is inferior to other products or services on the market. This can hurt your reputation and make it difficult to attract new customers.

How to Set Up Metrics for Your Project?

As a startup, it's important to have some sort of development metrics in place so you can track your progress. But with so many different stats out there, which ones should you be tracking? Here are five important development metrics that every project should keep an eye on:

- ► Number of new users/signups
- ► Number of active users
- ► Engagement rate

- ► Churn rate
- ► Customer lifetime value

By tracking these development metrics, you'll be able to get a better idea of how your project is performing and where there's room for improvement.

If you're using Google Analytics (and you should be), then you can easily track these metrics. Just go to the "Audience" section and then click on "Overview." From there, you'll be able to see all of the different stats that are important for your project.

But Google Analytics isn't the only tool you should be using to track your development metrics. In fact, it's important to use a combination of different tools so you can get a more complete picture of how your project is doing.

What is the KPI Goal for a New Project?

When you are a new business it is crucial to establish goals for development which can help you monitor your progress and make sure that you're on the right course to meet your goals for business. One way to do this is to set KPIs (Key Performance Indicators).

KPIs can be used to measure progress towards specific goals and objectives. They can be financial or non-financial, and can be tailored to the specific needs of your business.

Some examples of KPIs that you might set for your project include:

- Revenue growth
- Customer acquisition rate
- Churn rate
- Employee satisfaction score

It is important to choose KPIs that are relevant to your business goals and that you can realistically track and measure. Once you have selected your KPIs, you can start setting goals for each one.

For example, if your goal is to increase revenue by 20% this year, you would need to set a corresponding goal for each of the KPIs that contribute to revenue growth. This could include targets for customer acquisition rate, average order value, and conversion rate.

By setting KPIs and corresponding goals, you can

measure your progress and ensure that you are on track to achieve your desired results. The use of these and other metrics is described in more detail in the following chapters.

5 Recipes for Generating Startup Ideas

If you're stuck for startup ideas, try these five tips. I was able to gather these principles from my own practice and from the materials of the respected authors Fishbein[13], Golomb[14] and Shpilberg[15]. Start with what you and your team are especially good at. Think about something that you'd be excited to work on for the next 10 years. Also, think about something that has changed in the world. For example, if you're a sports enthusiast, think about something that would make it easier to play tennis. Then, look for things that have changed in the world since you were last active.

Start with what your team is especially good at

It is a common misconception that founders should start with a list of startup ideas that they can develop and then begin generating them from there. While this strategy may generate some good ideas, it can also produce many terrible ones that are perfectly viable and convincing enough to fool people into thinking that they can actually build a successful startup. As YC points out, "Coming up with a good idea isn't easy."

One of the best ways to generate startup ideas is to focus on what you and your team are especially good at. You may have an idea for a new product, a better way to market it, or a better way to use existing products and services. Start by identifying what your team is especially good at, and use that to generate startup ideas. By identifying what people are particularly good at, you will be more likely to generate a large volume of ideas from which to draw inspiration.

Developing a list of startup ideas based on your team's expertise is also a great way to improve your chances of success. For instance, you may think of creating a social network for pet owners. But it is rare that a startup is killed by a competitor. However, a competitor with a lock-in may prevent users from choosing between two services. By focusing on your team's skills, you'll be able to better prioritize your time and resources to make your startup a success.

Think of things you wish someone would build for you

Many successful startups started by addressing problems that people had. DoorDash founders wanted Thai food delivered in the suburbs, so they created a delivery service. Boom's founders wanted a delivery service but had no experience in the aerospace industry. In addition, PlanGrid was born because Apple invented the iPad. Both ideas were variations of existing successful businesses. The question is, what would you want to do in 10 years?

While the current problems that people face are an excellent starting point, you might also want to think about future problems that people will be facing. This may seem too far out of reach, but Elon Musk's SolarCity is an extreme example of this. While not for everyone, the lack of fossil fuels will soon become a problem, and he's taking steps to solve this issue now.

Look for things that have changed in the world

The best place to find startup ideas is not in a company, but in something that is missing. The people who are on the cutting edge of technology notice things that are missing - and that's the perfect place to start. Turn off all other filters, including the "could this become a big company" filter, and look for things that aren't available yet. You'll find plenty of startup ideas this way.

Another great idea for a startup is to find a niche that doesn't currently exist. This can be a gap or unmet need in the world, or even an annoying task at work. You should avoid aiming for startup ideas in industries that don't even exist - that way, you can profit from their decline. For example, if journalism has fallen out of favor, why not take advantage of that? There's probably still money in it, but it's likely that a new company will step in to replace it.

Ask people you for problems they want solved

To generate startup ideas, you must ask yourself the following question: What problem does everyone you know have? If you have the answer, you should then start a business to solve that problem. This approach is known as "do what you know." The advantage of this method is that you have some knowledge that can be leveraged to make a startup even better. After all, nobody has time to research everything, so you should start by asking the people you know.

The next step in generating startup ideas is to choose a problem that is large enough. Many startup founders fail to consider this question and therefore choose an idea with an insufficient market size. You must identify the size of the market before you pursue the idea. A big company may already solve the same problem as yours, which proves that there is a market for the product or service.

You can also combine two unrelated things to come up with an awesome startup idea. If you're good at problem-solving, you could start a business together with a friend or partner. Remember that a successful startup was never a unique product, but a product that solved a problem for someone else. If the two of you share the same vision, then your startup will succeed. Without compromise, however, you may end up with a flopped startup.

Look for industries that seem broken

If you're bad at coming up with startup ideas, try asking people what their biggest problems are. You'll be surprised at how many people don't have a good idea. This method is useful if you have specific expertise in an industry. If not, you can look at companies that have recently been successful and come up with a new variant. Standard

Cognition, for example, adapted the technology used by Amazon Go, and soon realized that every retail store needed to use the same technology. Though this approach won't yield the best ideas, it's a start.

If the market is full of mediocre products, this may be a sign of an opportunity. If there's no good coffee shop nearby, perhaps you can improve the experience by creating one. Or maybe you can't find an attractive cereal box in your local grocery store because it's too big. A startup that solves this problem is a good way to make money. But there are many more ways to come up with good startup ideas.

Key 10. Getting Started: Practice Steps

In addition to books, I like the startup accelerators[16] because they present short and clear actions. An example is an action plan like this, which has helped me out more than once.

Simple steps for first results

1. Have a process to get product out the door
2. Decide on a release schedule
3. Put someone in charge of product
4. Establish KPIs
5. Create a theme for the product cycle based on a KPI
6. Product meeting
7. Brainstorm new features, bugs, and tests

8. Sort each into easy, medium, or hard

9. Pick the hards first

10. Spec the ideas out and assign tasks

11. Shut up and get to work

12. Testing

It's not a fact that this cycle will work for your product, but I highly recommend having your action points. Needless to say, you don't need to repeat this exact process, in fact, you don't need to duplicate any aspect of it, but this is the most formal process that startups use to get their product to market. Aaron Ross[17], who focuses on the success of SaaS projects, has described a strong corroboration of these thoughts.

The 4 Steps to Preparing for a Successful SaaS Launch

In a conversation with my YC buddy Martin Brown, an experienced SaaS businessman, we shared steps and methods, and we came up with 4 Steps that are found in each of our projects. There is a division of somewhat similar steps in the works of John Higgins[18] and Bobby

Davis[19].

Historically, SaaS products were announced to decision-makers in a niche vertical market. Today, product-led growth focuses on attracting end users. This new model is more challenging and larger than ever before. To help guide your SaaS launch, follow this four-step plan. During the first phase, focus on building your cross-functional team and identifying key features.

Step 1. Developing a go-live checklist

Developing a go-live checklist for your SaaS product is crucial to your success. It will help you make sure your new product has everything your customers need and want, as well as eliminate potential bugs or hidden costs. The product demo and sales deck are critical to testing your new SaaS product before it goes live. Prototypes are great for evaluating the feasibility of a new feature or concept. Moreover, they can help you refine your product features.

In addition to a value-driven product, your SaaS application must also have the necessary security features, some of which I found in Gerard Blokdyk's book[20]. There are dozens of steps in this process, and they are all essential to the future success of your product. A coherent plan will help you avoid a mess in the development process and give you confidence throughout the process. By preparing a go-live checklist, you will ensure that you avoid potential procedural issues that can shut down your business.

An MVP is a product that shows users what they will get from using your SaaS product. The principles of MVP development are adequately described by Dr. Baker[21] et al.[22]. While launching an MVP is not a guarantee that you will have a successful launch, it will give you an idea of how complex it will be and how much time it will take to develop. To avoid a disaster, develop a go-live checklist that includes milestones and measurable timelines. The goal is to make your product launch a success, and your checklist will keep you and your employees on track.

Developing a go-live checklist for your SaaS product is essential for success. Beta testing allows you to ensure your product is viable and easy to use. Beta testing also helps you to find any features that need to be added and to determine the overall ease of use. After the beta launch, you should make changes based on user feedback. During the beta launch, you can also make changes to your code and fix any bugs that could hinder your users' experience.

Step 2. Identifying key features

There are several steps to launch a SaaS product, but the most important step is identifying the target audience. After all, this will determine the kind of messaging you need to use, which channels to use, and what tactics you need to use for your SaaS product launch. This is why you should conduct extensive market research to define your understanding of shipping performance (USP) and target users, as well as determine the tactics you should use to generate leads. This step can make or break your SaaS product launch.

Whether you're building a product from scratch or partnering with a company that has already developed a product, the next step is finding a product that solves a real customer problem. SaaS is all about solving a problem that people have. You might find a common problem that you've encountered. You'll then want to develop a solution for it.

One of the biggest mistakes new SaaS entrepreneurs make is thinking that everyone with a problem is a customer. That leads to a product that has too many features and may not address a single need. Furthermore, it's likely that some users won't ever use all of the features.

To avoid this pitfall, you should define clear KPIs and success metrics. These will help you formulate strategies and tactics to improve the product. Some other mistakes are described in the research of Rabia Haji[23].

During the validation phase, it's essential to determine the pricing model of your SaaS product. You need to evaluate whether your pricing model will work with your target audience, and you'll need to adjust it accordingly. If your product is new to the market, launching in beta could be the best way to test whether it works for you. Beta testing is an effective way to raise brand awareness and get customers excited about your product before you launch.

Identifying key features for a successful startup involves user testing and user research. A successful MVP helps you validate your assumptions and identify whether the market is ready for your SaaS solution. Once the MVP is ready, you can begin testing it by getting feedback from users and using a conjoint analysis to identify user preferences. In the end, you will have a working product that will be highly successful in the market.

Step 3. Building a cross-functional team

If you're building a SaaS app, you've probably heard about the power of a cross-functional team. The idea behind this type of team is to bring together members of different departments to work on a common problem. In theory, cross-functional teams are more effective because they can combat the effects of groupthink, a common problem where members of similar departments overlook different problems or assumptions. As an added benefit, a cross-functional team will be more likely to find ways to improve processes and solve problems by coming up with new and innovative ideas.

First, create clear expectations for each member. You'll need to clarify what each team member's role is and how they'll contribute to the overall success of the project. Having clear expectations for each member will allow everyone to work to their potential. For example, you should establish clear expectations and milestones to help the team communicate and reach a common goal. If the team members are not accustomed to working together, create a process where all team members will work as a unit.

A cross-functional team should be led by a product manager, with all stakeholders aligned towards a common goal and complementary strategies. A cross-functional team should be able to communicate the goals of the product to all team members in a consistent way. It can do so through webinars, internal training, and meetings. Remember, a team is only as strong as its weakest link, so you should communicate your objectives clearly and frequently to everyone in your organization.

As an entrepreneur, you must realize that the journey to a successful SaaS product is not a linear process. No matter how much research you've done, mistakes will inevitably happen. However, if you have a passionate team, there's a greater chance of success. Don't be afraid to ask questions and listen to feedback from current clients. After all, they'll be the ones who'll be the first to recommend your product.

Step 4. Listening to customers

To create a successful SaaS product, you must focus on listening to your customers. Listening to your customers helps you understand what they need and what they don't. You can use Google Analytics to find out what your customers want from your product. Then, you can use these insights to create a product checklist. Once you have your checklist, you need to conduct market research and understand your target market.

Research your competition - Usually, companies develop their products and services to fill a problem or a gap. Depending on your product, you should also conduct some competitor research to differentiate your product and make it stand out. The goal is to create an experience that helps your customers to get the most out of your product. Ultimately, this will increase your chances of success.

Create a great onboarding process - After signing up, your customers should be able to experience the ultimate product journey. MailChimp has an interactive onboarding process, which makes sharing a guide a breeze. The onboarding process must also provide real value to new users. Measure user engagement - Identifying where your customers are getting stuck can help you develop a better onboarding process.

Test your product - The customer success metrics you use to assess customer satisfaction will help you improve your product. By experimenting with your product, you can find out if it has bugs, features, or other issues. This will also help you plan the perfect launch based on what your customers are saying. Lastly, you should measure your current performance based on these metrics. If you can't do this, you need to create an internal metric system to ensure that your company requirements are met.

Customer success metrics are very different from support statistics, and depending on your vertical, you may have to use different metrics for determining customer success. Nonetheless, it's worth setting initial benchmarks based on your specific industry and customer type. Ultimately, it will help you get a better understanding of what your customers want in your SaaS product and improve your customer experience.

Tips for Creating a SaaS Pricing Page that Converts Visitors

Using an intuitive design is a key for your pricing page to convert visitors. Include value-based pricing and actionable information. If you want to make it more personalized, consider adding videos to your pricing page. Use these tips to create a highly-convertible pricing page. The next tips focus on the most important areas for your pricing page and are based on the practices of the client projects I supervise and those of other contemporaries in the field[24],[25].

Tip 1. Laying out pricing information in an intuitive way

Many SaaS companies offer several tiers of service and it can be difficult to lay out information on these pages. A successful pricing page is easy to navigate and clearly communicates features and prices. It should also give a visitor enough information to make an informed decision. Read the tips below to make your pricing page easy to navigate. The more time you spend on it, the more likely a visitor will convert.

The layout of pricing information is one of the most critical components of the sales process. While it is essential to make sure that the information is clear and easily accessible, not all pricing pages are created equal. To make sure your pricing page converts, incorporate a few strategies that have proven to be effective. Consider personalizing the tiers, limiting the number of options, and using color psychology to convert higher-cost offerings. Above all, make sure the pricing page includes a strong CTA that encourages the prospect to purchase.

Try a three-tier pricing model. Slack, for example, charges per active user, which can encourage customers to upgrade to a higher tier. Slack offers a discount for educational institutions and nonprofits, which shows that the company cares about goodwill. As a SaaS business, you need revenue ASAP, so it is important to encourage yearly subscriptions. Try highlighting the annual savings if applicable. Restaurant menus are also known to increase conversions.

If you have a SaaS product, you need to determine how to price it. The pricing model for SaaS products is similar to postpaid phone services, where customers pay according to their allowance[28]. Unlike large enterprises, small businesses usually have lower budgets. A SaaS provider should be able to cater to both of these types of companies.

Tip 2. Using videos for conversion optimization

Using videos on a SaaS pricing page can help your marketing team connect with your target audience and convert them into loyal advocates. Video marketing is a great way to attract new customers and improve your online presence, and Naike Romain outlines three ways video can benefit your business. Using video on your pricing page will help you make a personal connection with your audience, increase conversions, and increase your ROI.

Video demonstrates the value of the product and engages customers in an emotional way. More than ever, customers look to videos for answers to their questions and bolster their knowledge about a particular industry. In addition to helping potential customers make a decision, video allows you to personalize your company and show off your personality. It also helps your business stand out from competitors and fosters strong customer relationships.

Videos can also help your marketing campaign by communicating additional messages to your customers. For example, by using videos to introduce new products and features, you can encourage customers to subscribe to your mailing list. Likewise, you can use videos to explain how to use your products and services. Use them to demonstrate how easy it is to use them. By using videos on your pricing page, you can encourage customers to subscribe to your list or make purchases.

When using videos on a SaaS pricing page, make sure the headline conveys the product's benefits and why you should subscribe. Most companies use charm pricing, which ends in a non-zero digit. While this creates an illusion of lower prices, it still improves conversion rates. One example of this strategy is LiveReacting. This company offers a free trial to prospective customers, allowing them to test the product without committing to a monthly subscription. If your pricing page doesn't have a clear headline, use one of the main headings to reinforce your positioning. If you're selling a monthly subscription to your SaaS product, use the main headings to illustrate the benefits of your product.

Using videos for conversion optimization on a SaaS pricing page is an effective way to make your product stand out from the competition. The videos should be educational and give potential customers something to think about. Besides, they should help prospects solve their problems. Make sure to show them the advantages of using the product before they sign up for a free trial. This way, they will become more likely to subscribe to your product.

Tip 3. Including value-based pricing

Including value-based pricing on a successful SaaS pricing page is not an easy task. Developing a research methodology is essential to understanding customer behavior and what they're willing to pay for a solution. But if you don't want to spend a lot of time on research, it might be better to stick to cost-plus pricing and competitor-based pricing for now.

The benefits of value-based pricing are numerous. For instance, you can increase your operating profit by 11.1% by focusing on a small segment of your customers. Furthermore, this type of pricing model helps you build brand equity and combat churn. But it requires time and dedication. In addition, value-based pricing is a constant improvement process. Here are some of the benefits of value-based pricing for SaaS:

The pricing table is an integral part of a SaaS pricing page. Every SaaS company's pricing page is an essential source of truth for prospective and existing customers. However, it must contain certain key design elements in order to convert visitors to customers. Without these elements, website visitors will be less likely to make a purchase. Moreover, consumers want to see all the available pricing options. In order to create a pricing page that converts, you must include all the tiers of pricing available.

Including frequently asked questions on a SaaS pricing page does not mean you can ignore the importance of FAQs. FAQs are extremely important for companies with an established SaaS product. FAQs can be embedded within a pricing table, thereby giving prospective buyers greater clarity. Also, FAQs are useful to include educational content. You can use them to help prospects choose the best plan for their needs.

By incorporating value-based pricing on a Saas pricing page, you can boost your customer's lifetime value (CLV) and conversion rate. Traditional pricing strategies tend to ignore the willingness of the customer to pay. SaaS products are unique in their offerings, which makes them better suited to apply the value-based pricing model. By listening to your customers and making profit-maximizing decisions, you can ensure maximum conversions and high CLV.

Tip 4. Including actionable information

The most important thing to keep in mind when designing a SaaS pricing page is to include as much actionable information as possible. You can do this by including a drop-down module that displays additional pricing information and requires the user to take action. If you do not want to use a drop-down module, you can also add a table listing feature below the pricing table to make it clear if that information is included. However, it's not always easy to work with dense pricing information on mobile devices. Therefore, it's important to design your SaaS pricing page so that it appears identical on all devices.

Having a well-written SaaS pricing page is crucial to converting visitors into customers. While every business is unique, it's vital to include as much actionable information as possible to attract and retain customers. Fortunately, there are many different strategies for converting visitors into buyers. Here are a few of them:

Firstly, consider your target customers. It's crucial to ensure that your pricing structure is aligned with the values and personas of your target customers. It's also necessary to make your pricing plans transparent to your customers. Make it easy for your customers to know which pricing plan is right for them, and provide a link to your product's pricing page to make it even easier.

The most important thing to keep in mind is that a well-designed pricing page is the final destination of the customer journey. You want to convince your prospects to sign up and pay for your SaaS software. So, include information that will increase their trust in your product. Ultimately, you want to earn the trust of your visitors and convert them into paying customers. This is where the pricing page comes in handy.

In addition to presenting relevant information, pricing pages should also be designed to include a free trial option. If you do not include a free trial option, your visitors are more likely to decide to sign up for your free trial or choose another solution. Whether you choose to use a free trial or pay a monthly fee, a pricing page should provide all of the information a buyer needs to make an informed decision.

7 Ways to Attract First Users for Your Software Startup

While you may have heard about how important it is to find potential customers for your startup, this is not always the case. First of all, you need to identify a single decision-maker in the firm where you plan to sell your product. You should also find a point of entry for your product. For example, if the product costs $50 to $50,000, you might want to target business owners.

Once you have determined your target market, the next step is to find them. Spend some time brainstorming and researching potential customers. You can begin with broad categories such as age, income, and location. Then, you can break these down further. You should be specific enough to find potential customers, but not so specific that you lose track of the wider market. It's better to be too broad than too specific, as the first few customers will likely be your most profitable and easiest to convert.

When it comes to generating traffic, getting your first users is essential for the success of your startup. You will know how to find potential customers, reach out to online communities, and offer free "office hours" to solve a specific pain point. Once you have identified your potential customers, you will need to get them to sign up for your mailing list. You can use Facebook, Twitter, and email as a marketing tool to reach them.

Way 1. Start a personal newsletter

For small businesses, starting a personal newsletter can be a great way to build engagement and understand customer pain points. You can use your newsletter to address frequently asked questions, address FAQs, and feature customer testimonials or reviews. You can also embed a survey into your newsletter. The survey can be as simple as a one-question survey, or it can be longer, giving you actionable guidance.

To create a newsletter that is engaging and informative, use an interesting subject line. Make sure to draw readers' interest and compel them to click through and read more. Mail apps have character limits, so make sure to front-load the most attention-grabbing part of the subject line. This will increase your newsletter's open rate. If your subject line is short, consider making a template to save yourself time and energy.

When creating a newsletter, you should remember to follow CAN-SPAM and GDPR regulations. Make sure that your newsletter complies with these laws, and test it with email providers to see if it works. If your newsletter is well-written and contains relevant content, you can send it out to subscribers and gauge how it is received. It can be an effective way to connect with new potential customers.

While creating a newsletter, it's important to remember that most newsletter readers are busy and do not have time to read every single detail. Make it easier for them by prioritizing the information that is most relevant to them. Special offers, news about new products, and featured content are the best places to put them at the forefront.

This way, you will win their extended attention. After all, if a reader is interested in your newsletter, they'll most likely read the entire email.

Way 2. Host a contest

If you're running a software startup, you should consider hosting a contest to attract the first users. This is a great way to market your product or brand to a new group of people. A few ways to do this include contacting contestants ahead of time or offering them a free trial of your product. If possible, choose a contest that allows people to submit their images and videos.

Another great use for a contest is to conduct user research. By using your contest to collect consumer information, you can learn more about your target audience and make your product even better. For instance, if your software startup is developing a new feature, a contest can help you learn more about your users. For example, a contest may prompt people to answer a survey or participate in a poll. This information will be valuable later in the development process when you're able to improve your product.

When planning a contest, remember to keep your

audience's demographic in mind. Using a contest to draw in first users can help you refine your audience personas and ideal customer profiles. Be sure to tailor the contest to your target audience, and ask specific questions about them. Having a specific target audience in mind can make it easier to attract the first users your software startup needs.

Way 3. Reach out to influencers

When you reach out to influencers to attract first users, you need to know exactly who you're talking to. In a nutshell, you want to mention their name and introduce yourself as their "friend". You don't want to approach them with a sales pitch. But there are ways to engage them and get their attention. Here are some examples. 1. Identify influencers with a relevant audience

Influencers can boost your brand's visibility and credibility. Using influencers can help you build a connection with people who have similar interests and can endorse your brand. Influencers also help boost your sales and engagement rates. In order to identify influencers who are likely to buy your product, you need to understand your target audience and develop personas. Once you know your audience, start creating your influencer outreach strategy.

Start a blog. Bloggers love to hear from other people, so start writing on a popular blog. Ask if they'd be interested in hosting an ad or a product review. Don't forget to include your link in the content. Influencers can also be found on sites like Klear and Alltop. You can find influencers by following hashtags and checking their page views.

If you're trying to attract the first users for your software startup, you may want to consider reaching out to influencers in the field who share your goals. Influencers have large audiences and may be able to help you reach them through their followers. They also offer a unique way to promote your brand. They can help you build a loyal audience that will be willing to buy your product.

Way 4. Give the first part free

A free trial or freemium plan can be a powerful way to attract the first users for your software startup. This approach allows you to prove your product's viability, increase your market share, and attract investment. Once your prospects have validated their decision, they will be more likely to upgrade to the paid version. When your customers see the discrepancy between the value you promise and what they receive, they may hesitate to purchase your product. The free trial approach gives you a chance to fix this discrepancy and convince potential customers to upgrade.

If you are planning on offering a free trial or freemium plan, you should be aware of the different types of freemium plans. These plans let you offer a limited amount of use for free and charge for extras. While free trials are more affordable than traditional ad campaigns, they can help you reach more users and cut down on customer acquisition costs.

A free trial or freemium plan is the most popular way to attract the first users for your software startup. This plan allows users to sign up without providing their credit card information and uses a free trial version of the product. Once they have outgrown the free version, they upgrade to the paid version and enjoy all the benefits. Freemium models also help you collect feedback from early-stage users and improve your product in the future.

A freemium model is a good option for attracting the first users for your software startup if you are targeting a broad audience. But a free trial may not be the best option for your business if you plan to provide premium services.

This means that you must make the value of your free trial or freemium plan more compelling for your users to pay.

Way 5. Hire inbound specialists

Inbound marketing is an essential part of the marketing strategy for a software startup. Without a proper marketing plan, it is nearly impossible to attract customers and start generating revenue. To attract the first users for your software startup, you must know your target audience, identify their pain points, and create an engaging content strategy. You should also meet with clients to understand what makes them purchase your product. This will help you create relevant content for each stage of the buying process.

Way 6. Reaching out to online communities

Reaching out to online communities is a great way to introduce yourself to potential users. Create a profile that resembles the persona of your target customers and pose a question to your community members. Think about what you want to offer them as a member. Is it advice, deals, or a way to pick up new clients? Whatever it is, focus on answering that question. Online communities provide opportunities for people to connect with each other and learn new skills.

Reach out to online communities through LinkedIn, Twitter, and Facebook to promote your new product. These communities are full of people who are looking for products like yours and may have questions related to your niche. By fostering this organic networking, you can build a community of your target users. The key is to reach out to these users in several ways and make sure to choose the right channels. If you want your users to become members, start with the people who can give you the best advice. Ensure that the people you approach are relevant and have a high trust level in the community.

Once you've created your community, you can begin sharing useful content to help your members. Create a content calendar for your community that encourages members to make purchases from your site. Reaching out to online communities is one of the most important steps in creating your first users. But how do you promote it? Here are 7 steps to get you started:

Online communities are like virtual stores for your customers. By connecting with your community, you can tailor your content to their avatars and gain new insights about your customers. Your customers are the best sources of product feedback. And reaching out to these online communities will help you develop that relationship. So start building an online community today. You'll be surprised by the results. You'll be glad you did. You'll soon see how beneficial this strategy is to your business.

The most important step in building an online community is understanding what your target customers are looking for. Once you know this, you can build a community that suits your needs the best. Whether you're looking for a niche community for fashion designers or a group of coffee lovers, a community should reflect the desires of your target market. You don't want to create an online community with 1 billion members sharing experiences. You want a small, exclusive group of coffee lovers.

Way 7. Getting them to sign up for a mailing list

There are several ways to encourage new subscribers to subscribe to your mailing list. First, offer a freebie. This is the first email that new subscribers will see, and it's important to thank them for signing up. Then, include a way for new recipients to sign up without unsubscribing the original recipient. And, remember to include clear instructions for unsubscribing at the bottom of each email.

Provide some kind of value in return for their email address. Freebies work well because they offer an immediate reward for a signup. Another tried-and-true approach is to create complementary offers to gain a promotional partner.

Key 11. Measure and Track KPIs

Even a basic list of metrics has a decent number of options. Choose one priority metric for your project, ideally one that reflects 90% of the effectiveness of your actions. For me, that metric was MAU (monthly active users). The rest of the metrics I started to track in projects gradually as they developed.

When choosing a priority metric, you can use an indicator that answers the following questions from Adora Cheung, for example:

- Represents delivery of real value? (Active users, MRR, etc.)
- Captures recurring value?
- Lagging indicator?

▸ Usable feedback mechanism?

There are many key metrics to monitor as a software startup. These include ustomer lifetime value, CPC, customer acquisition cost, retention rate, and more. A successful software startup should measure these metrics to make sure its customers are happy and loyal. Listed below are 15+ of the most important metrics for a software startup. And remember, you can never have too many of them.

Most Important Metrics

▸ Retention
  ▷ Customer churn rate
  ▷ Customer lifetime value
  ▷ Inactive customers
▸ Revenue Churn
▸ CAC
  ▷ Customer contract value
▸ Payback period
▸ NPS (net promoter score)
▸ Email conversion
  ▷ CPL
  ▷ ARPA

- ▶ Organic vs paid users
- ▶ Referral rate
  - ▷ Rebuy rate
  - ▷ Sign-ups
  - ▷ In-app time
  - ▷ Customer renewal rate
  - ▷ Content referral
- ▶ Contribution margin
- ▶ Gross margin
  - ▷ Capital efficiency
- ▶ GMV
- ▶ ACV
  - ▷ Expansion rate
  - ▷ MRR (monthly recurring revenue)
  - ▷ Net churn
- ▶ TCV
  - ▷ Net expansion
  - ▷ Net churn rate
- ▶ Burn rate

Customer Retention

In a software startup, one of the most important metrics is customer retention. If you have a small customer base, you can measure customer retention by comparing your customer attrition rate with your customer lifetime value. In addition, you should measure customer retention by looking at the churn rate. I will show you how to measure customer retention and determine how much of a return on your customer's investment you can expect.

In today's competitive software industry, customer retention is a critical metric to measure. Customers are the lifeblood of your business and should be rewarded appropriately. Customer retention experts advise that your sales team should take the time to understand the pain points of your customers and their needs and that your marketing team should provide the product with a demonstration of its value. Your customer service team should be responsive to feedback and suggestions, and you should consider making some changes to your billing structure.

Your retention rate is the percentage of customers who purchase your product or service at least once. This may be a renewal of an annual subscription, the purchase of an a la carte feature, or an upgrade to a premium version. The average repeat purchase rate is between 20 and 40%. If yours falls below this number, then you need to reconsider your retention strategy. The key is to monitor the percentage of repeat purchases and figure out what is causing customers to abandon their purchase.

Customer churn rate

How to calculate customer churn rate in a software startup? There are several ways to calculate customer churn rate. For example, if your startup has 500 customers at the start of the quarter, and 50 of them leave because their contracts expired or because they had poor experiences with your customer service team, your customer churn rate is 10%. Alternatively, you can divide the number of customers at the beginning of the quarter by the number of customers lost during the period and divide it by 100 to get your total customer churn rate.

To determine your own churn rate, you must understand your customer base and the nature of your product. If you are targeting small businesses, then a 5% monthly churn rate is typical. But if you're targeting enterprise-level customers, then you'll need a lower churn rate, somewhere between 1% and 5% per month.

Customer lifetime value

The first step in establishing a KPI and metric is figuring out how to measure customer lifetime value. While the formula may vary from company to company, it is always helpful to keep in mind that a high-value customer is not worth losing as much as a low-value one. Another KPI and metric that is useful for software startups is gross margin. The reason why lifetime value is so important is because it determines how much each customer is worth to a software startup.

A company's CLV is measured as the average value of a customer over a lifetime. The figure will depend on the frequency and cost of purchases made by customers. It is particularly important if the product is sold on a subscription basis, as it allows for a higher profit margin. Similarly, it can help identify which customers are valuable enough to justify a large marketing budget. In addition, the CLV will also help determine which customers should be prioritized based on their lifetime value.

Inactive customers

Inactive customers are a great source of customer feedback. Ask them why they stopped using your product. This information will help you improve the product or customer service. Another important metric to consider is churn. Churn refers to the number of customers who stop paying for your product after a certain period of time. Some startups measure churn at 30 days, while others wait 90 days to avoid confusing inactive customers with those who have not yet stopped using their product.

One common mistake that startups make is treating active users as the primary metric. In most cases, revenue will be a multiple of active users. Revenue is another metric that may be difficult to track since it relies on strong network effects. If you are using the customer base as a KPI and Metric for a software startup, you may need to increase the number of active users. However, revenue is often the primary metric and 99% of startups use revenue as their primary metric.

Revenue Churn

It measures the number of new customers who purchase a service or product after the initial purchase. If you measure churn using MRR, you'll have the most relevant version. You'll also need to consider net promoter score, a useful metric for measuring customer satisfaction.

MRR churn is the most important version of churn

There are two kinds of customers: reference customers and lighthouse customers. Reference customers are the earliest adopters of your product, and their loss is more noticeable since their logos will appear on your invoices. Then there is involuntary churn, which accounts for 40 percent of overall churn and hurts your bottom line more than it helps your relationship with your customers. If your customers do not notice automatic disconnections, they may decide to leave the company for another option.

MRR is a crucial metric for software startups. It helps you understand your business and predict your revenue growth. You can calculate your MRR by adding up new customers and recurring revenue by subtracting churned revenue from the new MRR. Your net MRR is the difference between your new and old MRR. If your new customers outweigh your existing ones, your MRR will be higher than your churned revenue.

Customer acquisition cost

CAC is defined as a percentage of sales or marketing expenses. In the early days, you should adjust the number to take only a portion of salaries and expenses. Once you are making a profit, you can begin to measure the success of your business by looking at CAC. But before you start measuring this metric, you should be sure to adjust your other KPIs and metrics first.

If you're launching a software startup, you might want to consider using customer acquisition cost (CAC) as a key performance indicator and metric. This metric can help you determine whether your sales and marketing teams are working efficiently to attract new customers. Startups often spend substantial resources to acquire each customer. However, if these resources are not used wisely, the startup might find it difficult to turn a profit.

While small businesses should strive to limit their costs, it's important to consider how many new customers your business needs to survive. If you're spending $50,000 to acquire each customer, you'll only have acquired 70 customers. Using customer acquisition cost as a KPI and metric for software startups is crucial for assessing your success and determining where to invest your resources. But it's important to keep this information private. Don't burn any bridges or ruin relationships over CAC.

Customer contract value

One KPI and Metric that can help you measure customer success is the annual contract value. This figure represents the revenue you will make in a year from a customer. The calculation of ACV can vary depending on the industry, type of software, and target audience. It is important to note that ACV should not be confused with ARR, which measures recurring revenue over several contracts. In addition to ACV, ARR can be useful for determining the cost of a software startup's marketing and sales efforts.

ACV represents the average amount that one customer pays for a subscription to a product or service over a 12-month period. It should include fees, additional purchases, and upsells. The ACV should increase over time, meaning customers are paying more. Another KPI to track is Active Users, which measures how many active users you have. Make sure that you define active users so you exclude first-time users.

Payback period

The CAC Payback Period (also known as the CAC) is a fundamental metric that helps startups measure how long it will take to recover the costs of acquisition. It is an important KPI for software startups because it allows them to compare the costs of acquisition against their profit margins. While there are many reasons why this metric is important, a common misconception is that the payback period is a function of time. The actual payback period depends on a number of factors, including the size of the startup, the nature of its product, and the type of customers that it serves.

One of the best composite diagnostic metrics for product market fit is the payback period. Startups with shorter payback periods typically require less capital and grow faster. Publicly traded companies Zoom, DataDog, Slack, Crowdstrike, and Twilo all have short payback periods.

NPS

Net Promoter Score (NPS) is the willingness of consumers to recommend your product to someone they know. The NPS as a KPI and metric for software startups is becoming increasingly important as customers become increasingly impatient and cynical.

To make the most of your NPS, measure it regularly. The higher it is, the more customers will recommend your product or service. High NPS indicates that your customers are loyal and satisfied. And as they're your biggest advocates, they'll help you sell your product or service. In fact, a high NPS will save your software startup money on marketing. But how can you increase it? Here's how.

First of all, NPS is an incredibly simple metric to track. It's fast, easy, and cost-effective to implement. But be careful not to rely solely on NPS as the only metric. After all, Nokia missed the smartphone market when they switched to apps and touch screens. And you can't be too paranoid. Only those businesses can survive.

It can be used to predict customer churn

In the NPS survey, customers rate a company on a scale of 0 to 6. The highest scores are considered to be promoters, while the lowest scores are detractors. Promoters are likely to recommend the company to other customers, while detractors are less likely to do so. A company's NPS score may fluctuate, and the results should be analyzed to find out what is driving these responses. A good strategy to follow up with customers who flag problems is to send them personalized emails with special offers or discounts.

The NPS survey can provide valuable insights into a company's customer churn risk. Customer health score can help companies identify areas for product improvements and prioritize user requests. Customer engagement rate can help startups identify patterns of happy and unhappy users. It can also help identify problems in product onboarding and the adoption flow. With all these benefits, NPS is a crucial tool for software startups.

It can be used to improve customer experience

NPS can be a valuable tool in polishing the customer experience for a software startup. Its use can be attributed to the company's focus on UX, which is all-encompassing, which includes everything from online ads to legal terms of service. For Macaitis, success isn't simply determining whether or not a prospect signs up for Slack, but rather whether or not they recommend it to others. Ultimately, the NPS data can help with product development, both in repair of broken products and in creating new ones.

Customer experience is a vital part of any company, and

NPS is the best metric for benchmarking it. However, the importance of identifying key drivers of satisfaction is often overlooked. For example, one-third of customers will leave a company after experiencing one or two bad experiences. Even if a customer has multiple experiences, one or two poor ones can go months without being recognized. By focusing on customer experience, the marketing team can create a better customer experience for each individual customer.

Email Conversion

For software startups, email conversion is a crucial KPI and metric for a successful launch. This can be done by tracking a variety of metrics, such as cost per lead (CPL), average revenue per account (ARPA), and conversion rate. Emails that are personalized are highly engaging and have a higher conversion rate, as well as a 41% higher unique click rate. In addition to improving customer relationships, personalized emails also increase brand awareness and engagement, which ultimately increases revenue.

Cost per lead (CPL)

Many startups face difficulties in sales, marketing, and customer success. With a small budget, they must make every lead count. They must segment leads and improve lead volume, which requires paying experienced salespeople. These upfront expenses extend the payback period. Customer success is another challenge for SaaS startups. A bad customer experience will cost you money and eventually turn them away. Cost per lead can be calculated by dividing the cost of acquiring a lead by the total costs of customer acquisition.

The cost per lead is usually expressed as the total amount spent on generating leads by the firm. This cost is often used to determine how much marketing costs to generate a new lead. This metric is particularly helpful for marketing teams. It provides a way to measure the cost of acquiring new leads. The cost per lead metric can be calculated separately for each channel. However, it is best to calculate it for each channel separately.

Average revenue per account (ARPA)

ARPA, or average revenue per account, is an important KPI and metric for software startups. It allows you to determine when you're pricing your product appropriately and when to expand your business. The calculation is simple: divide your monthly recurring revenue by the total number of accounts. It's also important to note that customers can have multiple users. If a customer has multiple users, you can adjust the ARPA accordingly.

Often, a software startup will report its average revenue per customer in CAC. This figure will give an indication of how profitable the sales team's marketing efforts are. The goal is to increase this number by 30% within 18 months. In addition to paying the cost of acquisition by ARPA, software startups should also measure customer lifetime value (CLTV).

Referral Rate

A referral rate is an important metric for any software startup and should be a key performance indicator (KPI) for any business. A K-factor of 0.15 to 0.25 is considered good, and it will allow your team to evaluate your referral program and its rewards and incentives. Almost all businesses track website traffic, and it can be useful to track your growth over time.

Rebuy rate

In software startups, the referral rate can be an insightful metric. While it isn't necessary to track churn rate, understanding where new customers come from is a prerequisite to having an ROI conversation. Tracking referrals doesn't require expensive software or sophisticated analysis. All it requires is an honest question to evaluate the activities of your team. Referrals are a key source of new customers and the faster you can get them on board the better.

Sign-ups

The number of referrals is an important KPI and metric for any software startup. This number can be compared month over month and can be a useful indicator of demand. However, one should also keep in mind that the total number of sign-ups might not be indicative of the number of active users, and a significant number of those are not likely to use the product in the long term.

In-app time

In-app time is a great KPI to measure the amount of time that users spend within your application. While there is no universally recognized metric for every application, it can provide valuable insight into the content your users find most valuable. Using A/B testing and other methods to determine what your customers prefer, you can measure and improve your product. Here are five common metrics that any software startup should be tracking.

Customer renewal rate

Among the KPIs and metrics for a software startup, customer retention is important, but it can be difficult to determine what level of renewal is ideal. This is because it depends on many factors, including the type of service provided, the nature of the market, and the emergence of new competitors. In any case, an ideal Customer Renewal Rate (CRR) is at least 80%. SaaS companies usually achieve this level.

Content referral

Aside from revenue, content referral rate is an important metric for a SaaS startup. It is a key indicator for understanding user behavior, their interests, and churn. If this KPI isn't monitored, the startup will have trouble identifying why its users are abandoning its product. Another valuable metric to measure is in-app time, which focuses on the number of hours users spend using the product. It is particularly helpful for startups that depend on in-app usage to generate revenue.

Product referral

The key metrics for a SaaS startup revolve around customer acquisition, retention, and monetization. To make sure your software is a hit with users, you should track referral rates and understand user behavior. For example, website traffic measures the number of visitors to your site. Organic traffic refers to visitors who came to your website from search engines, while paid traffic comes from paid sources. Both metrics should be monitored closely to determine how well your startup is doing.

Contribution Margin

In order to understand how to measure contribution margin, it is necessary to understand the meaning of sales minus variable costs. The more you know about contribution margin, the more you can measure your startup's profitability and runway. Here are the reasons it is important to measure contribution margin:

Contribution margin is sales minus variable costs

In order to calculate contribution margin, a software startup needs to know its fixed costs and sales. A fixed cost is the price of a product. During the startup period, the company must invest in the acquisition of customers. This process often leads to a loss on the first sale. After that, the startup can expect to see a rise in contribution margin once the customer has been secured. The next step is to calculate the profit per unit sold.

The contribution margin is a crucial part of any software startup's financial strategy. The calculation allows you to fine-tune your pricing strategy and find the most profitable products and services. As a general rule, gross profit margin is the portion of revenue remaining after factoring in fixed costs and variable costs. The difference between the two is the proportion of variable costs that are included in the sales. Therefore, the software startup should pay attention to its contribution margin before implementing sales commissions.

It's a measure of profitability

Using the contribution margin to assess profitability will

help you perfect your pricing strategy and identify the best products and services to offer. Contribution margin is the revenue left over after subtracting the cost of goods sold and variable business costs. This metric measures the profitability of your entire business. You can also look at the profitability of specific products and services. For a software startup, the contribution margin will help you determine which products and services to offer.

Software startups can measure their profitability item by item to determine the amount of revenue they are generating. The revenue generated by a company is the product of the goods and services the company offers. Without revenue, a company cannot exist. Consequently, you should calculate the marginal revenue for every product or service your startup offers. When you produce one more widget, you will generate an extra $10 in revenue.

It's a measure of runway

When you run a software startup, you need to calculate your cash runway and use it to plan your financial future. This is especially important for VC-backed companies because they need this runway to accelerate hypergrowth and increase their valuation. To calculate your runway, you should know your gross and net burn rate. These are the two primary concepts in runway calculations and are critical to successful funding strategies and pushing for a higher SaaS valuation in subsequent rounds of funding. Regardless of industry, understanding your burn rate will help you prioritize revenue streams and manage costs.

Founders should pay close attention to their burn rate. This number is closely related to the amount of money that a software startup burns every month. Founders should look closely at what is causing their burn rate to increase or decrease and consider implementing changes before going through drastic measures. Founders should also consider what they are willing to compromise on if the runway is too short. You might even find that the details of your business can make you a better entrepreneur.

Gross Margin

A key metric for software startups is gross margin. Gross margin is the percentage of revenue left over after a company's cost of goods sold and expenses are deducted. This figure can be as high as 80% in the case of software startups. It is an important metric to follow in order to determine whether your business will be profitable. Early-stage startups do not have the benefit of economies of scale, so a high gross margin is essential to success.

Capital Efficiency

If you're a software startup, capital efficiency as a KPI and metric should be high on your list. As the most important item in a startup, cash is crucial. Without cash, your business will not survive. In fact, it's important to understand the difference between revenue and cash flow profitability to determine your SaaS's efficiency. Let's explore some of the most common capital efficiency metrics for software startups.

GMV

A startup should experience 100% annual growth. And once they hit that level, they should be able to scale up to a larger company. In addition to GMV, other metrics that software startups should consider include customer acquisition costs and recurring revenue.

Gross merchandise value (GMV)

If you're starting a software startup, one important metric to monitor is gross merchandise value. GMV is the total dollar amount of merchandise sold in a given period. Although it's not an exact representation of a company's revenue, it gives you a good idea of how your marketplace is doing. GMV can also be a helpful metric to track in comparison to your competitors. Depending on your business model, GMV may be more helpful than revenue as a KPI and metric.

ACV

One of the most crucial metrics for any software startup is the average customer lifetime value (ACV). ACV can be measured using a number of different metrics, including Expansion rate, monthly recurring revenue (MRR), and Net churn. Among these, the ACV should be the most important. However, a low ACV should be an important KPI for any software startup, as it indicates a lack of customer value.

Monthly recurring revenue (MRR)

The ACV is a valuable metric to monitor for any software startup. By understanding how your users perceive the quality of your software, you can strategize to maximize your revenue. However, it is useless without other metrics. ACV should only be used in conjunction with other metrics to accurately assess the performance of your software. Small adjustments in your ACV can lead to massive leaps in revenue. Here are some tips to keep in mind:

Expansion rate

The ACV is often considered a confusing metric for startups, especially when compared to similar companies. What exactly is ACV? Simply put, it is the sum of all completed contracts per year. You can find out how much ACV your SaaS business is making by adding up the values of each contract. Then, use this figure to make predictions about your company's future growth. Once you have an accurate CAC, you can then start evaluating your SaaS business's growth potential.

Net churn rate

A SaaS startup must track KPIs to ensure its continued growth and success. Metrics are necessary in all phases of the funnel, from acquisition to revenue. Missing a key metric can result in missed goals. Metrics help the startup adjust its growth plans as necessary.

Market reach

ACV is an important metric for software startups, but there are some key differences between ACV and ARR. The difference lies in how the company defines ACV. ACV is the average yearly value of subscriptions and includes both one-time and recurring fees. It is a momentum metric. ARR, on the other hand, measures annual recurring revenue. While ACV can be confusing, it does help software startups understand their growth.

TCV

While many startups rely on LTV to measure revenue, TCV reflects actual bookings and offers a more accurate view of a company's revenue potential. With this new metric, you can tailor your sales and marketing efforts to your customer's needs. This metric will replace LTV in many situations and could help you avoid costly mistakes. Here are some ways to measure TCV. Read on to learn more.

Total contract value (TCV)

One of the key performance indicators of a software startup is the total contract value or TCV. This metric measures the average contract value for a customer over a 12-month period. ACV should include fees, upsells, and additional purchases. It should also increase over time, indicating that your customers are paying more for your services. Another important KPI is active users. Make sure that you are clear on what constitutes an active user because you don't want to include first-time users.

When choosing metrics, make sure they are relevant to your business goals. While it is easy to choose metrics based on the rate of growth, it's more important to look for trends and benchmark them against other tech companies. To help you with this, I recommend a survey of 400 private SaaS companies, which provides deep benchmarking data and insights on growth and operations. These metrics will also help you put together a detailed business plan for your startup, which will be an excellent asset when pitching your business to VCs.

Net expansion

For software startups, using Net expansion as a KPI and metric can help you gauge the success of your product. While new customers are always welcome, it is equally important to keep existing customers satisfied. By analyzing the growth of your monthly or annual revenue, you can see whether your product has added value to your existing customers. If your monthly or annual revenue has increased, you can continue to increase your customer base.

Moreover, you can track other metrics, such as the number of monthly unique users and email subscribers. It is also a good idea to track the sales cycle, as acquiring new customers is four to ten times more difficult than retaining existing ones. To keep your customer base happy, you must focus on improving your engagement KPIs. In addition, you should measure how quickly your products and services are adopted by new users.

Net churn rate

For a Software Startup, Net Churn Rate can be an important KPI and metric. However, if you have a small startup, churn rates may be higher than what you would like. This is because startups tend to have limited budgets and their cash flow may be more volatile. But, once the company is established and has built up a strong rapport with its existing base, churn rates should decrease.

Another common mistake is the calculation of the churn rate. The problem with this metric is that it is not a real-time metric. You must wait for two months of data before calculating it. This is not a good idea, since it is impossible to know the number of canceled accounts before the end of the month. Further, you cannot report on the number of canceled accounts from September.

Burn Rate

A crucial concept for software startups, burn rate guides decisions related to forecasting, spending, and when to seek external investors. As a software startup, understanding the concept of burn rate will help you make better strategic decisions, such as how much to hire, where to locate talent, and when to seek outside funding. It is especially useful when the startup is early in its lifecycle.

Cost of growth

Burn rate is a metric that startups should closely monitor. It helps a company measure the amount of cash used per month. For example, if your company needs $100K in cash for a one-year period, your burn rate would be $50k per month. For every month you spend $150K on operating expenses, you will burn $50K. The idea is to compare your projected burn rate with actual costs so you can adjust accordingly. The higher the burn rate, the more you have to cut your expenses.

Another key metric is burn rate. If your startup is losing money too quickly, it may be time to raise more capital. The burn rate will help potential investors assess your funding health. For startups in the early stages, burn rate can be a useful indicator. It's also important to track your runway, which is the amount of money your startup has available in the bank before it runs out of cash.

Key 12. Stay Motivated

To ensure that your dreams do not collapse in on themselves and turn into a project that you can be proud of, consistency alone is not enough in the development processes. Being motivated and not burning out is a task you will expend effort on, but it will pay off. Following the experiences of reputable professionals[29] [30] described below will help you get the best results from your project.

Top Causes of Burnout in Software Developers

Burnout is a state of physical and emotional exhaustion that can be caused by long-term stress in your work.

Reason 1. Overworking

One of the most common causes of burnout in software developers is simply working too much. With the ever-increasing demands of the job, it can be easy to fall into the trap of working long hours day after day without taking a break. This can lead to exhaustion, both mental and physical, and can eventually lead to burnout.

Reason 2. Stress

Another common cause of burnout in software developers is stress. The job can be extremely stressful at times, especially when deadlines are looming and the pressure is on. This stress can take a toll on your health and well-being, and can eventually lead to burnout.

Reason 3. Lack of Job Satisfaction

Another cause of burnout in software developers is a lack of job satisfaction. If you're not happy with your current position, it can be hard to find the motivation to keep going. This can lead to feelings of hopelessness and despair, which can eventually lead to burnout.

Reason 4. Poor Work/Life Balance

A final cause of burnout in software developers is a poor work/life balance. If you're working too much and not spending enough time with your family and friends, it can be easy to feel overwhelmed and stressed. This can lead to burnout.

Watch for Burnout symptoms

The signs of burnout can differ from person to person, but there are three general dimensions that characterize it:

▷ emotional exhaustion

▷ depersonalization

▷ reduced personal accomplishment

Emotional exhaustion is characterized by feelings of being overwhelmed, drained, and depleted. If you're experiencing emotional exhaustion, you may feel like you're constantly under stress and that you can't keep up. You may also find it difficult to feel positive or motivated about your work.

Depersonalization is characterized by a sense of

detachment from your work. If you're experiencing depersonalization, you may find yourself feeling cynical or negative about your job. You may also feel like you're just going through the motions and that your work is meaningless.

Reduced personal accomplishment is characterized by a lack of satisfaction with your work. If you're experiencing reduced personal accomplishment, you may feel like you're not doing well enough or that you're not meeting your goals. You may also find yourself feeling discouraged or hopeless about your career.

Don't Panic if You're Already Exhausted

Most individuals, when they initially begin working, especially if they enjoy it, tend to go at warp speed with a lot of enthusiasm. However, over time, they do not notice that they are falling into the trap of burnout. When developers fall deeper into burnout, recovery is not simple. You must first acknowledge that no matter how much you tell yourself "you're fine," you know very well that you aren't.

1. Take some time off and find a new hobby. This will help to clear your mind and give you a break from work.

2. Don't overwork yourself. Learn to say no when you are assigned multiple tasks.

3. When you come back, start off slow. Don't jump back into work 8–10 hours a day.

4. Try a different language/stack and work with other databases or tools. This will help to reignite your passion for coding.

5. Change your coding environment. Move to a different room or try coding away from your desktop. These changes may help you to recover from burnout and get your passion for coding back.

The good news is that there are many ways to deal with it and prevent it from happening in the first place. You can start by taking a break, delegating some of your work, talking to your boss or colleagues and trying to find a way to enjoy your work again. Burnout doesn't have to be the end of your career. You can overcome it and come back stronger than ever.

How to Be at Your Best and Avoid Burnout

Tip 1. Take your mind off the code

Many developers find it difficult to take a break from coding, even when they're on vacation. However, it's important to take time for yourself and your family and friends. There are many ways to relax and rejuvenate outside of work, such as reading books, attending meetups or conferences, listening to industry podcasts, or writing your own technical blogs. Taking a break from coding every few months can help prevent burnout and allow you to return to work refreshed and motivated.

Tip 2. Rank the tasks

In order to prevent burnout in software development, it is important to focus on the most important tasks and eliminate those that are not impactful or take a lot of effort. This can be done by ranking tasks based on their impact and effort and then eliminating those that have low impact or require a lot of effort. Additionally, it is helpful to block social media sites and notifications while working.

Tip 3. Keep things fresh in order

To avoid software developers burning out and the necessity to keep things fresh. It is advised that developers dedicate 20% of their time to learning new technology and exploring different options. This will help keep them passionate about their work and improve their long-term career prospects.

Tip 4. Cheer on each new accomplishment

When you reach new phases or milestones in your development process, it's tempting to jump straight to the next thing. While it is certainly important to continue growing and evolving over time, it's also important to recognize what you've accomplished. When you do something great in your business or reach a specific goal, reward yourself in some way. Maybe host a party for your team, plan a quick trip or just buy something you've been wanting for some time. The ability to enjoy your achievements will keep you working toward your new goals and help you enjoy the process just a little bit more.

Tip 5. Take frequent breaks

Software development can be a demanding and tiring profession. It is important to take regular breaks throughout the day to avoid burnout. Sitting in front of the computer for hours at a time without a break can decrease productivity. Taking short breaks every hour and stretching or walking can help to rejuvenate the body and mind, and increase productivity. Talking to colleagues and asking for help can also be productive ways to take a break. Using a kitchen timer to break work into intervals can be helpful in maintaining focus.

Tip 6. Make sure you get enough exercise and sleep

In order to avoid burnout in software development, it is important to exercise and get enough sleep. It is also helpful to eat healthy foods and avoid caffeine after 2 pm. Additionally, it is important to reduce blue light exposure and keep the room temperature cool.

Tip 7. Follow an iterative development approach

Burnout in software development can occur when developers try to code an entire massive program without ever compiling or debugging any of it. This can lead to frustration and a feeling of being overwhelmed. To avoid this, developers should always follow an iterative development process on large projects, developing modules and testing them as they go.

Tip 8. Hire remote developers

If you are already facing the problem of programmer burnout, one solution is to hire remote developers. This will help to reduce the workload on your in-house team and improve the efficiency of your development process.

Tip 9. Read and watch positive stories

Find the right tools for you. There are websites, apps and other resources that can help you access a constant stream of motivation. Test out a few to find the best ones that work for your individual style. With the right tools in your arsenal, you'll be able to fight burnout and stay motivated no matter what.

Again, there are many ways to add motivation to your project and get inspired for the future. You can start with the described tips and enjoy your work. You can overcome a lot and become stronger than ever with each challenge.

Summary

If you have the right processes in place to develop and launch a project, you will succeed even if you work alone.

The advantages of working alone include fewer distractions, a more flexible work schedule, and complete control over the project. If you have limited time, you may want to consider working with a team.

Understanding the lifetime value of customers is critical to success in the software industry. To create a successful software company, you need to redesign the customer experience in terms of service and data flow.

The Business Model Canvas is a tool that helps startups and entrepreneurs develop a comprehensive model for their business. It consists of nine different components that include revenue streams, customer segments, value propositions, cost structures and key activities.

International expansion, high customer acquisition costs and lead generation are some of the most challenging aspects of this business model. However, with careful planning, adherence to tips and execution, these challenges can be overcome.

If you decide to engage a team, the best way to motivate your team and ensure their success is to keep communication open, let them know that their work is important, and celebrate successes together. Creating a positive and supportive work environment is key to maintaining a motivated and productive team.

One person acting as a mini-corporation with an understanding of their own areas of expertise and tasks will make it easier to delegate any authority when they are ready.

It is very important to have documentation that can be used by programmers and testers to ensure the quality of the software. Documentation for end users is also important because it can help them understand how to use the software.

The ideal place to look for startup ideas is advanced technology. You'll find a lot of things missing there — and it's the perfect place to start. With a little creativity and a look at the lessons of the past, you're sure to come up with and develop a great startup idea.

You can promote your online community by reaching out to others, offering a free service or creating additional offers.

It's crucial for startups to understand and track KPI metrics in order to make informed strategic decisions.

Apply the advices to keep yourself inspired and eager for a successful project release. Use positive sources of information and success stories.

Overall, following the advice in the book will increase your chances of building a successful software startup. Although it is not easy to build a business on your own, you can succeed if you focus on the right things.

References

[1] Lawson, J. (2021). Ask Your Developer: How to Harness the Power of Software Developers and Win in the 21st Century. United States: HarperCollins.

[2] Smyth, P. (2021). The Millionaire Software Developer: How To Use Your Software Development Skills To Build A 7-Figure Business. (n.p.): Booklocker.com, Incorporated.

[3] Rosato, J. (2021). Starting You Out As An Amateur In SaaS Sales: How To Be Successful In SaaS Sales: How To Sell Saas. (n.p.): Amazon Digital Services LLC - KDP Print US.

[4] Goodwin, P. (2018). Profit From Your Forecasting Software: A Best Practice Guide for Sales

Forecasters. United Kingdom: Wiley.

[5] Software Product Lines: Experience and Research Directions. (2012). United Kingdom: Springer US.

[6] Myers, D. (2020). Front-End Developer. (n.p.): BCS Learning & Development Limited.

[7] Tarlinder, A. (2016). Developer Testing: Building Quality Into Software. Netherlands: Addison-Wesley.

[8] Developers Road ahead: A Complete Guide For Software Architects To Succeed At Work And Life. (2021). (n.p.): Notion Press.

[9] Barker, T. T. (2020). Perspectives on Software Documentation: Inquiries and Innovations. United Kingdom: Taylor & Francis.

[10] Gentle, A. (2018). Docs Like Code. United States: Lulu.com.

[11] Leung, T. (2021). Beginning Power Apps: The Non-Developer's Guide to Building Business Applications. United States: Apress.

[12] Duvander, A. (2021). Developer Marketing Does Not Exist: The Authentic Guide to Reach a Technical

Audience. (n.p.): Duvinci, Incorporated.

[13] Fishbein, M. (2014). Where Startup Ideas Come from: A Playbook for Generating Business Ideas. United States: Createspace Independent Pub.

[14]   Golomb, V. (2018). Accelerated   Startup: Everything You Need to Know to Make Your Startup Dreams Come True From Idea to Product to Company. (n.p.): Time Traveller, Incorporated.

[15] Shpilberg, S. (2021). New Startup Mindset: Ten Mindset Shifts to Build the Company of Your Dreams. United States: Girl Friday Books.

[16]   Birdthistle, Naomi., Dunn, Steve., Busulwa, Richard. Startup Accelerators: A Field Guide. United Kingdom: Wiley, 2020.

[17] Ross, A., Lemkin, J. (2019). From Impossible to Inevitable: How SaaS and Other Hyper-Growth Companies Create Predictable Revenue. United States: Wiley.

[18] Higgins, J. H., Smith, B. L. (2017). 10 Steps to a Digital Practice in the Cloud: New Levels of CPA Workflow Efficiency. United Kingdom: Wiley.

[19] Davis Jr., B. (2020). Breaking the Code: Five Steps to a Life-Changing Software Development Job. United States: Lioncrest Publishing.

[20] Blokdyk, G. (2017). Saas Platform Security Management. (n.p.): CreateSpace Independent Publishing Platform.

[21] Baker, D. J. (2018). Getting to Market With Your MVP: How to Achieve Small Business and Entrepreneur Success. United States: Business Expert Press.

[22] Develop Your MVP: Mission Values Principles. (n.d.). (n.p.): AZEA WELLNESS, PLLC.

[23] Rabia Haji (2020) The 21 Common Fatal Startup Mistakes : And How To Avoid Them: Learn how to avoid the most common fatal mistakes on starting a digital business.. (n.p.)

[24] Kahl, A. (2020). Zero to Sold: How to Start, Run, and Sell a Bootstrapped Business. United States: Arvid Kahl.

[25] Dahlstrom, A. (2019). Storytelling in Design: Defining, Designing, and Selling Multidevice Products. China: O'Reilly Media.

[26] Barrow, B. (2017). Stakeholder Management: 50 Ways That You Can Become Brilliant at Project Stakeholder Management, Or How to Engage, Inspire and Manage Even Difficult Stakeholders. United Kingdom: CreateSpace Independent Publishing Platform.

[27] McManus, J. (2007). Managing Stakeholders in Software Development Projects. United Kingdom: Taylor & Francis.

[28] Swift, B. (2021). Idea to Acquisition: Creating SaaS that Sells. (n.p.): Amazon Digital Services LLC - KDP Print US.

[29] Cagan, M. (2017). INSPIRED: How to Create Tech Products Customers Love. Germany: Wiley.

[30] Ebsen, R. (2021). Founders In A Book: Inspiring Stories For Startups: How Startup Founders Make Money. (n.p.): Amazon Digital Services LLC - KDP Print US.

About the Author

Alex Gurkin is a founder and CEO at Friday CRM. He is a serial inventor with 15+ years of entrepreneurial and project experience. Prior to founding Friday CRM, Alex was co-founder of three startups sold and team leader of over 300 web-projects of his clients. In every business, Gurkin identified the fundamental need for a platform for companies to easily build communications with clients. Gurkin grew up in Siberia, started his first IT company in high school, and earned his MD in health information technology. In 2016 he moved to the USA where he founded own SaaS project and runs a consulting practice. He has taken part in accelerators for startups like Y Combinator.